MW00991516

The Financial Rescue Plan for Nonprofits

Leading Your Organization from Surviving to Thriving

by John Warren

Endorsements

"In *The Financial Rescue Plan for Nonprofits,* John Warren is, in effect, calling those of us in Christian leadership to heed Solomon's wisdom: 'Any enterprise is built by wise planning, becomes strong through common sense, and profits wonderfully by keeping abreast of the facts.' Those who do so may well survive— even thrive—in a climate in which Christian non-profits face increasing hostility from without and splintering from within. Fairly applied, the principles and precepts in this survival manual will re-establish the Christian enterprise you love upon a solid footing."—*Hank Hanegraaff, best-selling author and president of the Christian Research Institute*

"John Warren has been used by God to serve ACSI schools at critical junctures in their history. His banking background, business acumen, and ministry heart have brought a unique perspective and insight to assist Christian schools in fulfilling their mission. The Financial Rescue Plan For Nonprofits provides a thorough perspective on what John provides for Christian schools to accomplish their ministry and mission." *–Daniel Egeler, Ed.D., President, Association of Christian Schools International*

"With his expertise and experience in banking and finance, John Warren provided invaluable counsel to our board. His team literally brought our school from the brink of bankruptcy to financial health. Without John's help, our school would no longer exist." *– Paul House, Chairman, Board of Directors, Aurora Christian Schools*

"One of the best decisions we have ever made at Annapolis Area Christian School was to partner with John Warren and CFS Financial. First and foremost, John Warren is a committed follower of Jesus Christ. John's biblical priorities coupled with his intuitive insight into the banking/financing world, was just what we needed. I recommend John and the CFS team with great confidence and certainly with equally treat thanks for their selfless and superior work with AACS." *–Rick Kempton, Superintendent/Head of School, Annapolis Area Christian School*

"Faced with the crisis of a bank having foreclosed on the land we were leasing from an individual, Mr. John Warren found us through ACSI. Because of his fervent love for Jesus Christ and his fire-like determination to help ministries in financial distress, Mr. Warren and his CFS team gave us spiritual as well as financial insights that helped win us another year on the property. God is truly blessing the CFS ministry. We are glad John's banking expertise is being used to glorify God. We can wholeheartedly recommend Mr. Warren and CFS Financial." *–Dr. Thom Allen, Administrator, Grace Christian Academy*

© 2014 John Warren

All rights reserved. This book or any portion thereof may not be reproduced or used in any manner whatsoever without the express written permission of the publisher except for the use of brief quotations in a book review.

This book cannot substitute for professional advice. This book serves only as a general guide and cannot specifically address or remedy any individual situation. The author and publisher shall have no liability or responsibility to any person or entity regarding any losses incurred, or alleged to have incurred, directly or indirectly. No warranties or guarantees are expressed or implied. As the needs of every nonprofit are unique, if legal or financial advice is required, the reader is advised to consult with appropriate professionals.

Cover design by: Bob Ousnamer
Book design by: Dawn Staymates
Edited by: Kristen Stieffel

Printed in the United States of America
Second Printing, 2015
ISBN 978-1-941733-07-3

Requests for reprints may be submitted to the publisher:

EA Books, Inc
EABooksonline.com

Acknowledgements

Years of mentoring, both professionally and spiritually, are prologue to this book. I'm grateful to God for those who invested in me along the way, and I'm grateful for His saving grace in my life. My wife and daughter are sources of tremendous strength, love, support, and inspiration.

This book is dedicated to the thousands of school leaders, ministry leaders, board members, pastors, and business leaders who serve faithfully in Christian organizations throughout the world. You are the people who inspire me to do this work, and God uses your stories to encourage and drive me to work tirelessly on your behalf.

A special thank you to Paul House, Rick Kempton, Dan Egeler, Hank Hanagraaff, Mike Francis, Dr. R.C. Sproul, Burk Parsons, Renai Albough, and Tom Coletta. Your vision, teaching, support, counsel, and friendship have been used by God to mold my character and this work.

Finally, my thanks to the many banking professionals, board members, and regulators who invested valuable time and other resources into my life throughout my banking career. God is using years of professional development for His glory in Christian organizations throughout the world.

Contents

Introduction

A battle has been joined for the future of an important part of our great nation—a battle unseen by average citizens. The battle has been going on for years, but recently its intensity has forced Christian organizations to downsize or even close their doors.

In the past, placing the word *Christian* in an organization's name was enough. Even more subtle ways of identifying nonprofit schools or ministries as Christian worked. The people and revenue would come. In the 1970s and '80s, most Christian schools were perceived as offering higher-quality education than their secular competitors.

But boards and administrators became complacent, competitors retooled and reshaped into forms not previously seen, and the cultural departure from a Christian worldview intensified, creating a disastrous financial climate for many Christian nonprofits. This environment has created legitimate financial challenges, often exacerbated by self-inflicted wounds of mismanagement, lack of leadership, and weak organizational culture.

Government loan guarantee programs and other regulations have a bias against organizations involved in the exchange of ideals. Loan guarantee programs in both the Small Business Administration and the U.S. Department of Agriculture may not be used by churches, and they cannot be used by related organizations closely connected with churches. While this redlining around Christian organizations has been present for some time, it is enforced more aggressively today due to our culturally slipping closer to a worldview that is anti-Christian.

Complicating matters further is the financial crisis that began in 2008 and continues today. Financial regulators reacted to the bank failures of recent years and the near collapse of financial markets by tightening credit policy requirements at all U.S. banks.

This tightening, coupled with existing credit standards that have a built-in bias against nonprofits, restricts the flow of capital to nonprofits of all types.

So the anti-Christian cultural shift, plus banking regulatory changes, plus government loan program biases, plus the economic downturn adds up to an environment of intense financial crisis for Christian nonprofits.

My consulting practice focuses on Christian nonprofits from a financial standpoint. In this book, I explain the external economic environment, the current state of the banking industry as it relates to this group, and the organization-threatening financial obstacles faced by Christian nonprofits. I cite real examples to support and illustrate my findings, and I provide tools for the managers and boards of such organizations as they attempt to reshape their organizations for survival in this new economy. This book has written itself in a sense, and it tells a story that has to be told.

This book outlines many of the challenges faced by nonprofit leaders, and addresses best practices and advice I have developed over the course of consulting with hundreds of firms over many years in the banking and finance industries. Because my personal story is integral to my consulting practice, I've included it so you'll understand my professional background and my personal walk as a Christian.

Throughout this book I discuss banks, bankers, and bank regulators, and I want to be clear that most of them are hardworking, well-intended, caring, and competent people. Many of the negative outcomes described are the result of unintended consequences of regulations, policies, and procedures designed to solve problems or address issues. Many of these regulations and policies were put in place years ago, and others were put in place to address the financial crisis that began in 2008. Nonetheless these regulations and procedures affect nonprofits in ways that aren't always obvious, and this book exposes and addresses many of these beneath-the-surface issues.

Some will find my simple explanations of complex financial management concepts a bit unsettling. My challenge to managers and board members of nonprofits is to focus on excellence and the simplicity of effective financial management. As they can in so many endeavors, managers and board members of nonprofits can lose focus on the critical few areas of financial management while attempting to lead an organization during these challenging times. My hope is that this book will assist you in taking a more radical, focused approach as you lead your organization.

Throughout the book, I use the words "schools" and "organizations" interchangeably. Both references are intended to refer to Christian nonprofit organizations of all types. Given this difficult environment, my goal is to equip boards and other organizational leaders of these organizations with the tools necessary to survive and even thrive.

PART ONE
Diagnosing the Problem

JOHN WARREN

2

CHAPTER ONE
Recovery From Disaster

My consulting practice began with an amazing display of God's grace and guidance in my life and the life of a Christian school on the brink of financial collapse.

The banking industry has a long track record of mergers and acquisitions, and in the course of my career, I worked through many such transactions. I started my career in regional banking, but later became president of a newly chartered community bank in Central Florida. That institution was later bought by a large regional bank.

Community Bank: a small bank capitalized by local individual investors

Regional Bank: a multistate bank capitalized by institutions, such as Wall Street investors and firms; traded on a stock exchange

---

Twice more I served as president of community banks that were later acquired by regionals. The economy began to change in late 2007, but in my third community bank startup we were confident in our ability to create shareholder value, so we pressed ahead. Raising capital wasn't easy then, but we successfully raised $56 million.

The pressure on banks was palpably more intense than ever before in my career. Thankfully, we weathered the storm and quickly reached profitability.

Meanwhile, I began to develop an interest in leaving banking to do something more meaningful with the remainder of my career. I read several books about career change and prayed for God's direction. Privately, I began seeking counsel from friends about opportunities in ministry-related fields for someone with finance experience.

In the summer of 2011, a bank approached us with a merger offer. Although many failed banks were being acquired at that time, we were healthy and didn't think we would be attractive to a bank as strong as that one—in many ways the strongest bank in Florida. The top three executives are legendary in Florida banking, and they could have had their pick of acquisition targets. I would have put the likelihood of such a transaction near zero.

God's Call and Provision

During the effort to sell the bank, I searched the website of ACSI, the Association of Christian Schools International, for employment opportunities. I knew God was preparing a new future for me, and I wanted to do my part to prepare for the right opportunity. This was my first time on the ACSI site, and I simply browsed chief financial officer and other finance-type openings.

A school in Aurora, Illinois, had a posting for a financial management staff person that caught my eye, so I sent an e-mail to the designated party with the crudest of resumes attached. The position seemed uninteresting to me, and the location would certainly be a stretch for my family, but I wanted to at least begin the process of fine-tuning my search for ministry-related work.

A board member of Aurora Christian School called the following day, and our conversation was warmer than expected— almost as if we were old friends. Al said he was a human resources professional serving on the ACS board, and we immediately discussed the fact that I was overqualified for the position. He went on to describe the financial calamity ACS was facing. Their bank—the same large regional that had purchased our first community bank—had foreclosed on the school. Since I had a passion for ministry and twenty-eight years of banking experience, Al asked me if I would speak to Paul House, the founder of ACS, about their troubles.

My conversation with Paul the following day was troubling. Paul is a man of God who had founded the school forty years earlier. Through a series of events that started with the donation of a large tract of land, he found himself and his organization in deep, treacherous waters.

As I learned the details of board and parent attempts to negotiate with the bank, as well as the bank's posture and all that had already been done to finalize the foreclosure, I began to sense that the school was likely to fail.

When used in a foreclosure, a stipulation agreement basically sets forth the terms of an orderly handover of property. ACS had already executed such an agreement with its bank. The agreement called for ACS to vacate the property at the end of the 2012 school year, and it specified in detail the terms of the event and the legal transfer of title of the property. ACS had about 800 students, and I became overwhelmed with the prospects of the families involved losing this school.

Every contact with Paul and the board revealed a passion for Christ and a desire to do the right thing. I fell in love with these people and their school, but I knew there was little I could do to help. Our family began to pray for ACS and its survival.

I participated in several ACS board meetings by phone, and I routinely talked by phone with Colette House, the school's superintendent. She would often tell me of correspondence or phone conversations with the bank, and I would advise her on how to handle each issue that surfaced.

She would say, "But the banker said in an e-mail I received two months ago that was impossible."

I would respond with, "We are going to pretend we didn't hear him, and we're going to ask him for this concession as if we expect it."

Colette is very intelligent, so I could hear the tentative, almost condescending acceptance in her voice when she said, "Okay, I'll call him."

Over time, the bankers began to make small concessions which eventually led to a small opening in the doorway toward crafting a mutually acceptable deal.

We had several conference calls with the school's attorney. He, too, had given up hope on any resolution other than vacating the building at the end of the school year. After months of coaching Colette, consulting with the board, reviewing correspondence, and participating in phone conversations, I began to lose hope for the school's survival.

My good friend Tom Coletta, a former banking colleague, had a bad experience with his first entrepreneurial effort due to factors beyond his control, and he closed the business at about the time I gave up on ACS. Tom called me a number of times seeking counsel on his next career steps, and I eventually suggested that he consider contacting a company that works with financial consultants to help them set up private practices. Tom had years of banking experience, he is very intelligent, and his communication skills suit him for financial consulting. He attended some training in California and opened his own consulting practice the following month. He sought commercial customers who were experiencing challenges with banking relationships and project financing.

Early on, Tom was frustrated with the challenges of growing his practice, so after asking their permission, I introduced him to the folks at Aurora Christian School. When Tom called me two months later asking me for any referrals I might be aware of for his business, I asked him if he had contacted ACS. He had not. In fact, he had forgotten the name, and I had to repeat the story and provide Colette's contact information again. I told him they were likely to fail, but they had won my heart and I wanted to do as much as possible to assist them. Tom contacted Colette, and Tom and I began new negotiations with the bank while also seeking replacement financing.

The following six months were frustrating. Although the bank agreed to give the school another year at their facility, despite our best efforts, the bank would not negotiate with us. Further, we encountered all sorts of loan sharks and predatory lenders in our effort to locate replacement financing.

At this point, our bank's sale was under way, Tom was building his business, and I was working hard to manage the bank and complete our merger. My contact with ACS and Tom was limited, and I spent many evenings discussing various options and strategies with Tom and Colette. There were many points in the process at which Tom, Colette, and I wanted to give up on resolving the conflict with the bank and refinancing the school.

Incredibly, six months later we had located a lender and negotiated successfully with the bank to reduce the amount owed from $20 million to $12.5 million. The deal even included a provision for reducing the debt further to $8.5 million through the sale of a piece of vacant property. The process was as painful as any multilayered negotiation I had ever encountered, and the favorable resolution was the result of God answering our prayers and employing our finance and negotiating skills in an amazing way.

On October 31, 2012, the ACS transaction closed, and Colette House was able to tell the school family that God had answered prayer.

On the same day, Tom completed a project with a church. He called me the next day and asked, "Do you think God is trying to tell us something?"

When I expressed confusion, Tom explained that he wondered if God was trying to show us that we should work together to focus his company on ministry-related financing issues. I actually laughed out loud and thought little more about his comment until the following week, when events altered my negative response and changed the course of my life.

Paul House called two days later to tell us that five schools had heard the ACS story and expressed an interest in talking with us about their financial issues. Conversations with the schools referred to us by Paul revealed a pattern of financial calamity among Christian schools across the country. Each discussion seemed to scream for the need for our company to work with these schools. Every inquiry led to more referrals, and within just a few days' time we were talking to over twenty schools.

Meanwhile, Colette had invited us to a praise service at ACS the following Sunday afternoon. Tom had a conflict and couldn't attend, but I decided to attend the service as a courtesy to Colette, Paul, and the school's board. Colette explained the basic format of the meeting and asked me to prepare a short talk. I flew up to Chicago and back on the same day.

As the room began to fill, I could sense the energy among the administration, faculty, and families of ACS. The families looked as if they had just been rescued from drowning, and I heard story after story of how important the school is in the lives of families in Aurora. I wasn't quite sure what to expect that day, but I hadn't expected the gathering to feel so profoundly powerful.

I shared the story of the school's financial rescue from my perspective, explaining that at several points during the process my assessment of the probability of ACS surviving had been close to zero. I knew that God had answered prayer and had used a couple of bankers from Florida to salvage a school that honors Him and educates children for His kingdom. The service had a sense of beauty and reflected God's faithfulness and power.

When my talk ended, I stood at the back of the auditorium. Colette made some closing remarks and Paul prayed. Paul House can preach a sermon, and he gives one the sense that God is going to cause revival when he prays. I was struck by the beauty of his prayer and the significance of the work we had done in the lives of the families in Aurora. Person after person stood in line to shake my hand after the service ended. I received appreciation from teachers, staff members, and parents of students. This was the first time in my life that I could recall God using my financial experience in a ministry setting in such a clear way. I was overwhelmed with the significance of this moment.

A twelve-year-old girl walked up and extended her right hand to me for a handshake. She shook my hand and looked me right in the eyes and said, "Mr. Warren, my name is Susie, and I'm in eighth grade here. I just want to thank you for saving my school because I love it here, and I want to graduate from this school. I love God and I love this school. Thank you for everything you did for us."

After thanking her and telling her that I have a daughter her age, I began to cry as she walked away. I knew then that God had placed me there for that moment, and that he had me fly to Aurora for this day to meet the families of ACS and to meet this little girl. I began to think about the multigenerational impact of educating children in a Christian school environment. I met parents who had been students there and were now building their own Christ-following families and educating their children at Aurora Christian School. I thought about the multiplication effect and the incredible ramifications for the community, state, and nation from the work of this one school.

When I reflect on the particulars God used to draw me to this work, I almost tremble in amazement. It would be foolish to think for a moment that these events could have happened randomly.

First, I hired Tom Coletta as a lender at a regional bank early in my career. He agreed to join me in our first community banking effort, and we both invested all our financial resources in that endeavor. Our first two community banks sold at very profitable margins, and we started a third bank during the economic downturn.

In the midst of all that, I had survived a bout with colon cancer, which God used to increase my resolve to focus my life on following Christ. Cancer taught me to take time and focus on relationships. I learned that eternity matters more than temporal pursuits. I learned that trusting Christ for salvation is the most important decision we can make.

Against incredible odds, God used our expertise, life experiences, and hard work to rescue one school from financial disaster. Referrals from Paul House helped us identify the broader need. We saw a pattern of financial decline, banking challenges, and related struggles by nonprofit companies throughout the country. Referrals poured in, and we have since helped many schools, churches, and other entities resolve critical financial challenges threatening their survival. This wonderfully daunting, rewarding, challenging, complex work is really just beginning.

It is as if God thrust us into this incredibly tenuous world of nonprofit financing at a time when the need is critical and resources are scarce.

This book describes many of the trends we have observed, issues we see many nonprofit organizations facing, and practical information on key areas of financial management that will benefit organizations of all types.

We see a number of common financial themes among schools, churches, ministries, and other organizations. My hope is that you will see God's hand at work in your organization as you employ these strategies and tactics.

As in the Aurora story, the themes of financial hardship in organizations throughout the United States are incredible. Schools, churches, and ministries on both coasts, in the heartland, and north and south share internal and external challenges, commonly failed resolution efforts, and common management and board challenges.

I have had the privilege of working with schools with as few as 55 students and as many as several thousand, from California to Florida to Massachusetts and across the Midwest. I am blessed to have consulted with organizations which were on the brink of failure but are now thriving. My assignments have ranged from the routine to the humanly impossible. Banks which were adversarial to schools have completely reversed course and made decisions favorable to the schools, and boards which were acrimonious are now working together to improve culture and organizational strength.

When I have talked to my tenth company during a week, and the financial struggles of the organizations appear to be insurmountable, I often pull back and think about the implications of salvaging just one small organization. I then replay in my mind the list of organizations we have helped, and this gives me the strength and tenacity to carry on. This is the impetus for writing this book. Here you'll get practical information that will benefit your organization as you navigate the treacherous waters of this challenging environment.

CHAPTER TWO

From the First Signs of Trouble to Financial Crisis

My friends often overrate my financial predictive ability, largely because they think raising capital and operating a bank requires or confers an understanding of the economy and an ability to predict its future. This is not the case, as I have proved several times.

The most recent occasion of this was in November of 2007, when I agreed to raise $55 million in capital with several friends to start our third community bank. Many of you probably sensed that the economy was slowing at that time, but we moved forward with the same zeal that had accompanied our previous efforts.

My first clue that we were experiencing a downturn came in the spring of 2008, when regulators began scrutinizing our strategic plan and expressing concern over our aggressive growth projections. My second clue was the fact that it was more difficult to raise capital than previously. I expected to raise the entire $55 million, based on our track record of turning a $1 investment into $11 through just two banks over a seven-year period. My third clue was the reports of large banks selling off huge blocks of commercial real estate loans at deep discounts.

It was clear that we were headed into a recession, and it was also clear that a residential bubble was bursting. I remember learning about big banks taking discounts of 70 percent to offload commercial real estate loans, and I remember the sobering sense that what was happening was significant and negative.

I remember holding a reception during September of 2008 while bailouts and the potential collapse of several financial giants were being discussed. The purpose of the event was to complete our capital-raising efforts. In the first thirty minutes, I heard story after story of financial concerns from prospective investors. We eventually exceeded our $55 million goal, but we had to work twice as hard for double the amount of time that we anticipated. So I am no stranger to financial and economic denial.

After working with Aurora Christian Schools and Paul House's initial round of referrals, I saw patterns among the nonprofits we were trying to help. In most markets, the Christian school industry has always had financial challenges. The breadth of families attracted to Christian education almost necessitates financial tension between the amount a school can charge for tuition and the cost of educating a child. The level of this tension varies from market to market, and this funding gap has historically been bridged by a combination of discounts, scholarships, and corresponding cost cuts and fundraising. While there is no typical Christian school or nonprofit ministry, there are enough common themes regarding this funding gap and the resultant financial challenges that I believe I can summarize many of the challenges in an overview that every nonprofit manager and board member can relate to.

Another common theme is a "build it and they will come" mentality. This was sometimes accompanied by a "build it now and we will figure out how to pay for it later" approach. In the past, aggressive lenders and a competitive banking environment made it possible for schools and ministries to borrow money on terms that could only be met based on projected income growth. Many organizations looked at their growth trajectory and created plausible cash flow projections based on the indefinite continuation of a rising trend in enrollment and tuition income.

At many nonprofits, large donations of cash, land, and buildings compelled boards and leaders to grow rapidly. In some cases, designated gifts had stipulations which necessitated building new campuses and buildings. In other cases, boards felt their stewardship duties required the utilization of these gifts.

Almost every nonprofit I encounter has experienced elements of difficulty with respect to revenue challenges, changes in the banking environment, and the general financial health of their organization. Here's a sampling of the kind of comments I hear:

- We thought we would fill the new building because we had been growing at X percent per year for several years.

- Our bank had always been easy to work with, so we didn't scrutinize the terms of our last renewal carefully.

- We thought our fundraising would continue and even improve, and we certainly didn't see a dramatic decline coming.

- Our bank was great to work with until they were acquired by a much larger bank.

- Looking back, we shouldn't have taken on so much debt, but now we're stuck with payments which are crushing our school.

- Our families have been devastated by the economy with the loss of jobs, and we can't raise tuition as we had planned.

- Our area is not a high-income neighborhood, so we're hurting more than most, and there is no way we can increase tuition or raise funds.

- Our bank has the upper hand, and they are going to foreclose. They already warned us repeatedly and raised our fees and interest rates.

The reactions I hear from organization leaders to these financial challenges also indicate a sense of struggle with acceptance:

- We have to cut costs to survive, and we can't raise revenue.

- Our bank will work with us because one of our board members has a good relationship with a local bank.

- Banks don't want the publicity of a foreclosure on a church or Christian school.

- There is nothing we can do, because we can't pay our debt even if the payments are cut in half.

- The only expenses we can control are salaries, and we have cut them by X percent.

- We didn't make our last payroll, but we are collecting tuition for next year, and in two weeks we should be able to pay 50 percent of the amount we owe our teachers.

- We can't raise funds in our area because we don't have any rich people here.

- We can't tell our parents about our financial crisis because they will panic and want to pull their children out of our school.

- Our last superintendent was fired because she didn't think we had a financial problem. Or…

- Our last chief executive officer was fired because he didn't understand business, and our board felt he was irresponsible and it was just time for a change.

The human condition makes it difficult for an organization to pause and objectively evaluate its strategic and operating condition and plans, especially during a financial crisis or severe economic downturn. For-profit companies—wherein an owner, a group of partners, or a group of shareholders have a direct and significant financial interest in the organization—struggle with maintaining clear thinking in times of financial stress. When those serving on the board of the organization are volunteers from all walks of life, sharing a sense of mission but not owning a direct financial interest in the organization, that effect is exacerbated.

A for-profit board has a fiduciary duty to act in the best interest of the shareholders. A nonprofit board comprising the very best available members often falls into a sort of cognitive dissonance trap, as the implications of decisions don't directly affect their own self-interests. Having flesh in the game in the form of a direct financial investment engenders a level of care and involvement, with the self-interests of the individuals on the board connected to the self-interests of most other shareholders.

The nonprofit board member of a Christian organization has a stewardship duty that goes beyond the fiduciary duty required by secular board involvement. Making kingdom-impacting decisions is a far weightier assignment than simply protecting the value of an earthly investment in a company. Nevertheless, nonprofit boards often function with less focus, intensity, and clarity than their for-profit counterparts.

The Nonprofit Funding Crisis

The Aurora Christian School experience, along with subsequent engagements with other schools and my own observations during this part of my banking career, reveal a funding crisis for nonprofits in general and Christian nonprofits in particular. Our nation has an anti-Christian media and cultural bias today that seems to be intensifying. While this bias is not the subject of this book, it is important for Christian organizations to recognize that this cultural bias exists. Whether the issue is permitting for new buildings, applying for governmental variances, or seeking funding for loans, Christian organizations often face taller mountains to climb than secular peers.

A second element of the nonprofit funding crisis is the banking industry and its regulatory environment. Banks have a built-in credit bias against loans secured by "special-use" real estate, and many Christian organizations have this type of property.

Schools with classrooms and gymnasiums are considered special use because they aren't easily converted to other uses in the event of foreclosure. Churches with large auditoriums and sanctuaries are likewise not readily convertible to alternative uses. Bankers consider these facts in a portion of their underwriting. A focal point of bank loan underwriting is the "what happens if something goes wrong" scenario. Most banks wouldn't want the negative publicity of foreclosing on a Christian organization, and they go out of their way to appear to be the kind, gentle, friendly hometown bank. However, in the collateral analysis that occurs when banks evaluate a loan, they penalize special-use properties from a valuation standpoint. This is typically done by the appraiser, but the Christian organization will typically experience challenges to their own value assumptions of their property based on the perception that most of these properties have single or special uses.

An additional banking bias exists due to the very definition and structure of a nonprofit. Banks prefer ownership by individuals. Banks want to have individuals with a high level of accountability running the organization, owning the organization, and guaranteeing the organization's debt. The nonprofit sometimes has a person with a high level of accountability running the organization, and this is a positive bank underwriting characteristic. However, nonprofits don't have stockholders or owners per se, and they don't have individuals who guarantee the organization's debt. Bankers rarely discuss these issues with nonprofits, but you can be sure that a lack of shareholders and the absence of loan guarantors are seen as significant negative factors.

From a debt-funding standpoint, the anti-Christian cultural bias, coupled with these negative characteristics, produces an inherent disadvantage for Christian nonprofits. One might argue that these factors have been in place for many years, but the financial crisis of 2008 added a third element of negative banking bias toward nonprofits which not only intensifies the underwriting criteria but often provides banks an incentive for getting out of existing loans to these organizations.

For those real estate loans that are under increased scrutiny in the post-2008 regulatory environment, banks must have a minimum amount of capital reserved to compensate for loan losses—those that are not repaid. In addition, banks now must stratify their loan portfolio based on the loan and collateral risk type. This means every commercial loan secured by real estate restricts future lending, based on how much capital the bank is required to hold in reserve.

These restrictions mean it is often attractive for a bank to exit a higher-risk loan, which requires setting aside a larger amount of capital, in favor of booking a new loan with shareholders, guarantors, and real estate collateral that has broader use possibilities.

Courteous treatment by the bankers, a less-than-direct communication of the bank's displeasure with the nonprofit organization's banking relationship, and the fact that both bankers and their clients tend to avoid trouble in the short run, can result in confusion at the nonprofit.

A "special assets" officer from a large bank who was clearly attempting to exit one of my client schools actually said, "We like the school…they are the party that wants to refinance and leave us." When I asked if this meant she didn't want the school to refinance and leave the bank, the officer said, "No, at this point we think it would be best if they left."

While there are good people with good intentions in the banking industry, there are also those who embrace their corporate culture to the point that they deny sound reason. I urge every nonprofit to consider the facts rather than the rhetoric they hear from their bankers. If the bank is raising rates and fees, declaring default at every opportunity, initiating collection or foreclosure procedures of any sort, or even probing "problem financial areas" aggressively, the nonprofit should at least consider that the bank might not be communicating as directly as they should.

The aforementioned challenges are real and pervasive, but all is not lost for the nonprofit experiencing these funding challenges. Non-bank funding sources are available, and this book outlines both internal and external remedies available to Christian organizations facing these challenges.

CHAPTER THREE
The Red Flags

The financial warning signs that should alert the board of a Christian nonprofit to a potentially serious financial decline encompass matters of liquidity, leverage, and solvency. These warning signs manifest in the following ways:

- Consistent cash flow losses or significant net income declines

- Inadequate cash flow to cover debt payments or operating expenses

- Liquid reserves less than 150 days' worth of operating expenses

- Any bank action indicating discomfort or adversarial action, including rate and fee increases

- Declining enrollment or declining gross revenues

- Changes in the external competitive environment

- Material declines in annual donations

- Accumulation of debt to cover operating shortfalls for multiple years

- Human resource problems such as turnover and poor morale

The ups and downs of running a school, church or business will cause temporary disruptions to liquidity, leverage, and solvency to be sure. Discernment is required by board members and organization leaders to determine the velocity and duration of declines in financial condition.

> **Liquidity:** The amount of an entity's assets that are in cash or relatively easily converted to cash.
>
> **Leverage:** In the nonprofit context, this usually refers to the amount of debt that has been incurred as contrasted with fund balances.
>
> **Solvency:** The degree to which an organization is able to meet its short and long term obligations, including loan payments.

Consistent Cash Flow Losses or Significant Net Income Declines

The mission of a nonprofit requires the investment of surpluses in activities and assets which will facilitate accomplishment of the mission. It is therefore important for nonprofits to focus on operating surpluses and deficits. While operating cash flow is the primary concern of the board in terms of financial performance, provision for capital expenditures must also be made. This is often accomplished through a capital expenditure reserve fund. If the organization doesn't have such a fund, it should at least have a line item in its budget to address these issues, based on the aging and obsolescence of assets and the costs of anticipated repairs and replacement. Most schools I work with use an operating budgeting methodology, but few also budget anticipated capital expenditures.

Failing to repair equipment or replace obsolete assets to achieve solvency is not the achievement of solvency. Budgeting and planning approved by the board must be comprehensive and must include all repairs and maintenance. Having said that, stretching supplies and managing asset depletion is certainly part of the role of management in any business environment, and by suggesting that these items be planned for appropriately, I am not advocating for the perfect maintenance of plant and equipment. In most settings, that would not be cost effective.

The board and management should ask tough questions if cash flow losses are occurring and income is declining. Ask the obvious question—why?—and then probe a couple of layers more deeply. This will almost always reveal data which indicate whether the issue is peripheral or pivotal. "I would like to see the detail behind…" is not a threatening comment and should be construed as constructive. See Chapter Six, "Board Management," for more about climate control in the boardroom.

Exceptions that would explain declining cash flow trends might include intentional down-sizing or service elimination. In the case of a school this could include changes to the campus, elimination of certain electives, adjustments to athletic offerings, and other intentional downsizing activities.

Wisdom is required when determining the significance of a cash flow downturn. For example, the timing of expenses and revenue can sometimes create the appearance of a cash flow concern when revenue was actually received after the financial statement cutoff date. Conversely, improper accounting of income or expenses can cause cash flow to appear acceptable when revenues are recorded in a prior period or expenses are delayed until after the statement cutoff date. The proper timing and accrual of income and expenses are important elements of a sound accounting system that produces financial statements which are accurate and meaningful for management and the board.

Bookkeeping trickery is not productive, and third-party reviewers such as banks can see through the more common of these games by observing a multiyear cash flow history. Although most readers of this book would consider it unthinkable, several Christian schools in my consulting experience have experienced various iterations of accounting manipulation. In one case, the administration attempted to deceive the board with limited disclosure and using the sort of timing malfeasance described above. In other cases, the entire organization has been willing to improperly account for revenue and expenses to give the appearance of solvency when solvency is in jeopardy. This tactic isn't right under any circumstances, regardless of the audience or intended effect.

When cash flow concerns arise, board members and senior managers should probe deeply to determine the cause of adverse changes and whether or not the change is anticipated to be chronic. I have listed this concern first on the list of warning signs because cash flow deficiencies can erode liquidity and net worth, thereby threatening the organization's survival.

Inadequate Cash Flow to Cover Debt Service Obligations or Operating Expenses

The adequacy of current and projected cash flow must also be considered by management and the board. Cash flow adequacy should be stress-tested by the nonprofit in anticipation of factors that might adversely affect the company's ability to meet its operating requirements and repay its debts.

There are really just three ways to affect cash flow:

- Increase or decrease income.
- Increase or decrease operating and capital expenses.
- Increase or decrease debt payments.

In most nonprofits, income is received from operating activity and donations. Expenses are typically either operating expenses or capital expenses, which are required to maintain assets necessary to accomplish the organization's mission.

Most people have an acute pain-aversion system. Managing an organization properly means that at times, acute pain will occur. For example, in a school with declining enrollment and fundraising, cutting operating expenses might be on the list of short-term remedies that management must employ. With payroll being the most significant operating expense category in most organizations, salary reductions, staff reductions, and benefit limitations are sometimes the only tools available to management when addressing cash flow shortfalls. The acute pain of taking the appropriate action in a timely manner is morally prudent, and it also eliminates the chronic pain associated with other, less direct approaches.

No matter how accommodating your staff appears to be when you advise them that payroll will be two weeks late, organizational credibility declines when failure to manage proactively (acute pain) necessitates this action (which becomes chronic pain). Your staff isn't likely to tell you they are leaving at the end of the year because their perception of the quality of the organization declined as a result of these practices, but this is often the case. Further, they aren't likely to tell you that they discussed their concerns with others in the school family or in the organization's sphere of influence, and you probably won't immediately learn of the resulting reputational damage.

Expense cuts are painful, and tuition and other price increases are difficult. The middle class has been forever altered by this "new normal" economy. As a result, fundraising has never been as challenging for organizations as it is today. However, the acute pain of addressing these issues proactively pales when compared to the chronic pain of denial or manipulation. Telling a roomful of teachers "everyone is going to have to take a 10 percent pay cut for the following reasons until revenue improves" is horrible. But telling the entire staff "payroll won't be released on time for the third consecutive pay period" will potentially do far more damage.

I encourage boards and managers to think of these matters as a much larger story—one that involves image, credibility, and reputational risks. While the execution of these strategies and tactics requires deft delivery and discernment, I hope to increase your awareness of your organization's tendency to accept chronic pain and denial over acute pain and awareness.

Cash flow adequacy should be tested in anticipation of changes in interest rates and payment schedules, and adverse changes in economic conditions should also be considered when stress testing cash flow. Most of my clients find themselves in a reactive rather than proactive position in this regard, but the more forward-looking organizations are doing their financial management planning one to five years ahead.

Liquid Reserves Less Than 150 Days' Worth of Operating Expenses

There is no perfect formula for establishing liquid reserves, but the optimal number isn't much lower or higher than 150 days' worth of operating expenses for your organization. Liquid reserves are essential to the safety and soundness of any organization. Please don't think of liquid reserves as squandered or underutilized resources. Think of them as a necessary safety net.

Saving for a rainy day is a concept with a lot of merit for nonprofits. If we learned anything during the recent economic downturn, we learned that conditions can change quickly and more dramatically than we previously thought possible. Think of liquid reserves as funding that will buy the organization time to react in the event of unforeseen negative circumstances.

I don't believe this economy is presently healing. I believe it is stagnant, and nonprofits are in for a protracted period of financially challenging conditions. Organizations with proactive, well-planned strategies and tactics, plus a long-range, innovative focus will thrive. Those which are reactive and myopic will remain in denial and will struggle or even fail.

Whether through donations, expense cuts, or income enhancements, I urge you to build and maintain cash reserves. Reserves are not only a safeguard against unexpected cash requirements, they also allow an organization to seize opportunities requiring cash. And if a reserve accumulation strategy is wildly successful, excess reserves can be used for other purposes—even scholarships, endowments, or additional ministry opportunities.

Any Bank Action Indicating Discomfort or Adversarial Action, Including Rate and Fee Increases

This misunderstanding of the banking industry and banking relationships is perhaps the most common theme I see in nonprofits. The banking industry, including some private funding sources, is unique, and its ambiguity to outsiders is intentional in several respects.

The Great Depression and other periods of financial uncertainty, including the recent financial system troubles, have produced layers of regulations which make the banking industry difficult to understand for even sophisticated nonprofits.

The banking industry itself has struggled in recent years. For example, the state of Florida had 320 state-chartered banking franchises in 2007—today that number is closer to 210. With failures accounting for a significant amount of attrition in the industry, the regulatory environment for today's bank is much more restrictive than it was even six years ago. Both regulatory bodies and banks themselves have a confidentiality mandate. These requirements relate to the safety and soundness of the industry and the protection of customer data. Confidentiality requirements can make it difficult for those outside of the industry to fully understand banking and the relative strength of a particular financial institution.

Banks make money by taking deposits and lending them to qualified borrowers who pay loan rates exceeding the amount the bank pays in interest on its deposits. This "spread" is typically about 4 percent in a high-performing bank. The margin or spread covers operating expenses, including credit losses and other costs of doing business, and it provides a profit equivalent to about 1.2 percent of total assets at a typical high-performing bank. Banks also make money by charging fees for services. Monthly account fees, activity charges, and fees for ancillary items like credit card services are common sources of income.

Banks are challenged by the requirement to mark assets to their market value. A bank's assets include its buildings and equipment, but the primary asset of every bank is its loan portfolio. A bank's loan portfolio is marked to market, or adjusted to reflect its current value, through a system that calculates the appropriate level of reserves the bank must hold in the event of a loan loss.

The Details of Marking to Market

Bank loan portfolios are marked to market value through a loan-grading system that looks at loan type, industry, collateral type, and other risk factors. It prescribes a general reserve formula for each loan grade. When industry, collateral or performance concerns exist, a bank might adjust the loan balance with a specific reserve— usually based on a decline in the financial condition of the borrower, a decrease in the perceived value of the collateral, or both.

Collateral values come from an estimate of the property's true market value. It is likely that a loan with a balance of $10 million, for example, would be carried on the books of a bank for $10 million minus a general reserve, and minus a specific reserve if other risk elements exist or the collateral's value declines.

In a sense, banks may keep two sets of books. One set is the loan operating system, and the other is the bank's accounting system. So even if your loan balance has been valued below its actual principal amount, the loan system will continue to reflect the actual amount of principal owed. In our $10 million example, if general and specific reserves mark the market value down to $9.6 million, the loan system will still reflect a balance owed of $10 million. But the accounting system, which the borrower does not have access to, would carry the loan at a value of $9.6 million.

Complicating matters even further is the bank's macro portfolio management system. In recent years, to avoid the additional risk caused by banks' concentrating on too small a number of loan collateral types, regulators have added rules regarding a bank's loan portfolio relative to its capital position. The bank's loan portfolio is stratified by collateral and loan type, and the total of each collateral type is contrasted with the bank's capital to determine whether the bank has exceeded the recommended regulatory capital ratio for a particular loan type.

For example, real estate serving as collateral might be owner occupied commercial real estate, and the regulatory requirement might be that the total of the loan portfolio in this category not exceed 300 percent of its capital balance. Other, higher-risk categories such as investment real estate property might have a limit of 100 percent of a bank's total capital. If a bank's loan portfolio exceeds the required limit relative to its capital, the bank can either increase capital or reduce its loan portfolio in the offending loan type.

Increasing capital is difficult in this environment, and it lowers the value of current shareholders' stock. Therefore, most banks address this challenge by downsizing the offending elements of their loan portfolios. Many Christian nonprofit organizations find themselves in these undesirable loan categories, and consequently they become exit targets of their banks.

Banks also have their own credit culture. Recently, a number of national banks decided to exit most of their nonprofit real estate portfolios. Banks use industry default history, financial indicators, and other risk factors to manage their credit appetite, and they use various exit tools to rightsize their loan portfolio accordingly. For example, a bank will examine its nonprofit or its single-use real estate portfolio more carefully if it has a loss history that indicates such scrutiny is warranted.

Because customers don't have access to this information, it might be confusing for a customer that has enjoyed a lengthy, mutually beneficial working relationship with a particular bank only to find that the bank becomes adversarial and expresses an interest in exiting said relationship. This often occurs even when there has been no negative change in the borrower's financial condition, further confusing the borrower and its board.

Another factor that has made banking for Christian schools and other nonprofit organizations much more challenging in recent years is the special-purpose nature of the properties used as collateral. Such properties have limited market appeal, and banks tend to favor collateral types that appeal to a broad market segment. Office buildings, for example, may be used by a wide variety of users in a number of industries, but school buildings and churches typically require significant alterations to offer the same versatility.

The Christian school and church default rate—that is, the rate at which they fail to repay their loans—has also increased in recent years. Because these organizations have no shareholders, and therefore the loans have no personal endorsers or guarantors, banks insist on additional scrutiny and a higher level of underwriting. This can be confounding to a board member who runs a medical practice as a primary care physician. Her banker often solicits the practice for additional loans and even invites the physician to special events and entertainment venues. This well-meaning board member struggles to understand the differences between her owner-occupied medical office building and the single-purpose school building occupied by a much weaker nonprofit entity which has no shareholders.

My consulting history includes many cases of such board member attempts at assistance in which the nonprofit learns the painful lesson that their organization just isn't as desirable to a bank as a for-profit business might be.

Complicating matters even further is the fact that the school isn't experienced at managing a complex banking relationship, so the banker's common courtesy is construed as likely loan approval, and only when the banker finally comes clean at the end of a long, painful underwriting process does the school realize their loan wasn't ever likely to be approved.

The typical school's banking relationship might look something like this.

The school was founded many years ago, and they are still using the bank that made the first loan with which they acquired their original campus. The relationship has been a very strong one. In fact, the bank may sponsor a club or team at the school—at a minimum they place an ad in the yearbook or playbill.

The banker and the chief financial officer or superintendent have become friends, and the banker's children might even attend the school.

The bank was acquired by a larger bank eight years ago, and the friendly hometown banker assured the school that nothing would change. The banker even met with the chairman of the board of the school to tell him about the merger the day before the merger was announced because the relationship between the bank and school is a familial one.

The school has experienced enrollment declines in the past, but that has stopped. Fundraising has been more difficult, and financial performance has declined a bit, but the school still pays on time and financially breaks even—or better. The school has adequate cash reserves, and although new equipment purchases had to be placed on hold, the school is building some momentum and enrollment is up by a few students over last year.

Then, strangely, the bank declines a request for a small increase to the existing loan. When the bankers met with the school they seemed very positive and promised an answer in three weeks. After week three, when the superintendent called the banker to ask about the approval, the banker didn't take the call.

That call wasn't returned for several days.

After another call from the school, the banker answered and said the loan was declined.

In some cases, the banker doesn't even respond, hoping the school just stops asking for an answer.

A board member enjoys a strong relationship with another local banker at another bank, so when he hears of the difficulties in getting an affirmative answer from the school's bank, he calls his banker and has a great conversation about the school's situation. The banker even says, "I would love to handle this for you."

The banker then meets with the school's board, the credit process above is repeated, and the answer is either not given or, after some time, it is negative.

Then the current bank calls because they have finally reviewed the school's prior year audited financial statements, and they have concerns about operating performance and several ratios. They schedule a meeting with the board, and this time the banker brings his boss from the headquarters of the new bank. While the conversation includes pleasantries, the tone is much more subdued…even somber. The banker explains that they simply have some concerns, and they ask to see the school's budget and plans to remediate the concerns at a subsequent meeting.

After that, the bank sends letters to the school demanding a remedy for the default caused by the school's financial ratios failing to comply with the loan agreement. The school meets with other banks and even non-bank entities. The non-bank entities want to collect fees upfront for "underwriting" and their interest rates are high.

The banks are courteous but all eventually decline the loan request. The current bank initiates foreclosure, or at least becomes aggressive in asking the school to exit. Board meetings turn contentious, and the school becomes consumed with the prospect of losing its facilities.

Sound familiar? I have observed various iterations of this story played out in organizations large and small throughout the country. I offer some practical advice on banking relationship management in Chapter Seven, but for now, understand that this is the single most misunderstood element of financial management in most schools and churches.

The loan loss reserve system often allows banks to discount loan amounts—said differently, this means they can compensate schools and churches for leaving the bank so the bank can meet its strategic and regulatory goals.

Seeing the warning signs associated with your organization's banking relationship can be challenging, and navigating the treacherous waters of addressing a banking relationship that is showing signs of becoming adversarial can be very stressful, especially when board members are treated differently by the bankers they are associated with.

I often encounter schools who believe their banking relationship is healthy even though the bank is sending exit signals at every turn. Reading the banker and managing the banking relationship require artful execution and can significantly influence the financial condition of your organization.

Declining Enrollment or Declining Gross Revenues

Almost every school I work with has experienced or is experiencing a drop in enrollment or other revenue challenges. A handful of schools, however, don't have this problem or have managed it very well. Declining enrollment over consecutive years should concern the school's board. Other than planned or explainable short-term attrition, declining enrollment indicates a problem in marketing, image, value proposition, cost, quality, or some combination thereof.

Homeschooling is here to stay, and charter schools are allowed in most states. The external environment is challenging from a competitive standpoint, and it isn't going to improve. School boards have to decide how they're going to stand out—how their school can charge more tuition and be considered worth it by their constituents—or how they're going to improve their value proposition over time by hiring better teachers or promoting the right person to principal, or by employing a public relations campaign to remind prospective clients of the strength of their value proposition.

> **Value Proposition:** The summary of goods and services offered by an organization and how they will meet the needs of the organization's clients.

Boards and administrators must work together to own this issue. Seeing declining enrollment or declining gross revenue as uncontrollable or inevitable is not acceptable. All hands must be on deck working to build the school's image and strengthen its marketing effort. Some schools are growing while most are struggling to hold onto students. Don't allow the tide to reduce your expectations. Resolve to fastidiously work together to create your own microenvironment. I'll address this subject further in Chapter Ten.

A brief example of a school that has led the way in revenue maintenance is an East Coast school that had its share of turbulence, including leader turnover and even litigation. The school's board successfully raised tuition over the past eight years through a methodical process. They lost 15 percent of their enrollment during this period, but they increased total revenue as a result of the tuition increases.

I certainly don't advocate aggressive tuition increases for most schools, and I appreciate the desire of most schools to educate students without inadvertently discriminating based on ability to pay. The school in my example works with families on payment plans and offers discounts based on need, but they have admirably managed revenue well, and consequently they were able to weather a complex adversarial banking relationship. Their liquidity, leverage, and solvency positions allowed them to refinance their debt last year. We negotiated favorable terms on a twenty-five-year fixed-rate, tax-exempt bond and paid off their bank. This wouldn't have been possible without the effective revenue management strategies that their board put in place years ago.

I realize the importance of mission—in fact, mission drives me to do the work I do. But financial survival depends on sound management. Without it, the mission isn't going to be fulfilled.

Changes in the External Competitive Environment

Schools, churches, and ministries have historically been protected from some of the competitive pressures experienced by the private, for-profit sector. Christian schools have competed with each other and with public schools. This environment has changed over the past ten years.

Homeschooling has swept the United States by storm. According to the U.S. Department of Education's National Center for Education Statistics, the number of school-age children (5 to 17 years old) being homeschooled is currently about 1.7 million students.[1] The National Charter School Resource Center says charter schools are operating in 41 states and Washington, D.C.[2] Public schools are scrambling to improve their quality, and voucher programs add options for parents and children. The supply and demand factors faced by Christian schools have changed the landscape forever, and schools which haven't adjusted their quality initiatives, pricing strategies, marketing strategies, and other elements of their strategic plans are likely to fail in this competitive environment.

The playing field isn't level when two-thirds of the competitors have a cost structure that is a fraction of that of the typical Christian school, and the other third offers lower costs and better flexibility. Delivering, managing, and pricing the way we have always done will no longer work. When facing an environment with commodity-like market characteristics, perceived quality is the key differentiator that will improve competitive position. Boards and managers must observe the macro environment well to note changes in the competitive landscape.

Material Declines in Annual Donations

Most of the entities I work with receive donations from several sources. The more fortunate nonprofits have a base of wealthy individuals who periodically make large donations. Sometimes this giving is done annually or systematically. At other times it is either sporadic or based on communication of a specific need or growth opportunity.

Almost all the nonprofits I work with receive donations from middle-class families who support their causes. These families give sacrificially because they have been affected by the

---

[1] "Parent and Family Involvement in Education, from the National Household Education Surveys Program of 2012," National Center for Education Statistics, http://nces.ed.gov/pubs2013/2013028/tables/table_07.asp

[2] "Understanding Charter Schools," National Charter School Resource Center, http://www.charterschoolcenter.org/priority-area/understanding-charter-schools

organization or, at a minimum, they recognize the value of the organization. These donations range from a few dollars per month to thousands of dollars per year, and they almost always come from families directly influenced by the organization or from their relatives and friends.

The third source of income for most nonprofits is project or event fundraising. These occasions include galas, golf tournaments, dinners, and small-product sales. They range in efficacy from breakeven to earning several thousand dollars. I rarely hear of a project or function that nets more than $20,000, but a few projects have enjoyed greater financial success.

Giving to Christian schools, churches, and ministries has declined in recent years. This is largely due to the impact of the economic downturn on the middle class. Even wealthy individuals have become gun-shy about giving because of economic uncertainty, and the middle class has lost capacity for giving due to unemployment and underemployment, depletion of cash reserves, and a loss of confidence in predicting future cash flow.

Almost without exception, the organizations I work with have been hurt by this decline in giving. The more resourceful companies have increased the number of fundraising projects or devoted more effort to fundraising. However, the typical organization which has relied on fundraising to fill its operating cash flow gap is unable to do so at historical levels.

The dilemma has become, "We can't raise tuition or other revenue, we can't raise funds as we have in the past, so what do we do?" When the alternatives for growing revenue—increasing enrollment, raising tuition, increasing fundraising from individuals, and increasing fundraising from projects—aren't effective, what can the board and management do? Costs can only be cut to a certain point without materially damaging quality, and at some point, revenue must be improved if the organization is to survive. I address practical, creative, and completely out-of-the-box alternatives in Chapter Eight.

Accumulation of Debt to Cover Operating Shortfalls for Multiple Years

Organizations accumulate debt for multiple reasons. A common theme among nonprofits is simply the inability to service existing debt. The accumulation of debt typically develops because loans were taken out to enhance facilities based on enrollment or service levels that have now declined. Said differently, the expected ability to repay debts was based on an overestimation of revenues.

Making matters worse, many organizations facing cash shortfalls were initially able to borrow from banks, board members, and other friends of the organization, and that debt has simply spiraled out of control. For a significant number of nonprofits, the prospect of ever realistically servicing or retiring debt at current levels is just not feasible.

Making matters worse still, banks have tightened credit policies and loan administration practices, making money harder to borrow. The once harmonious relationship enjoyed by many organizations with their banks has become acrimonious. Not only is additional credit, which would at least avert the current cash flow crisis, not available, but draconian measures by banks to manage and even exit current loans have jeopardized the solvency of thousands of nonprofits.

The problem can be as simple as reaching the end of the organization's ability to make its loan payments on time, or as devastating as accumulating more debt than the entire organization's net worth, including goodwill or entity value.

Boards and managers are often faced with a wall that cannot be climbed, yet they know the mission of the company is incomplete. They see the need for their services growing, but they increasingly feel that their future is doomed. Many of my initial contacts with these organizations start with "you don't understand, we are going to have to close unless (insert humanly impossible event) occurs."

These challenges are real, and I certainly do understand the stress and desperation associated with attempting to manage this level of financial crisis. However, I will later offer practical tools for survival that might seem impossible or unconventional, but have been successfully employed by many of my clients in recent years.

Boards and managers must not give up, and must work expeditiously to avoid the flight-or-fight tendencies these stressful circumstances can evoke. At a root level, it is important for the organization's leaders to recognize that the accumulation of debt to cover operating shortfalls for multiple consecutive years indicates a threat to solvency that must be addressed.

Human Resource Challenges Such as Turnover and Poor Morale

The final warning sign during financial decline is one of the most consequential and less obviously visible. Schools and other organizations go to great lengths to maintain and assess morale. Turnover is tracked from year to year, and various indicators, such as test scores and survey results, are also used to assess quality and organizational morale. In my experience, however, the toll of financial distress on the human resource in an organization is almost always underestimated.

I have actually heard board members and administrators say they don't believe their staff and families know about their financial issues when the organization is on the brink of financial collapse. Not only do your employees know more than you realize about your financial calamity, but your other constituents know and routinely communicate their concerns with each other and with others in your community.

I often discuss with clients the fine line between making constituents aware of the challenges so they can become part of the solution and the sense of panic and subsequent cascading decline that can start when communication goes too far or isn't handled well. While answers to these challenges aren't as objective and concrete as we would like, understand that people know more about your organization's financial issues than you realize, and your failure to communicate will allow the storm to grow.

Turnover is a problem for all organizations. The cost of turnover is difficult to measure, and culture and organizational strength are often threatened by turnover. Managers and administrators will naturally explain away turnover and morale issues. This is due, in part, to the denial stage of the grieving process, and it is also due to the natural, human desire for self-preservation. We all avoid acute pain, as mentioned earlier, and we embrace chronic pain by default. No one enjoys confronting a morale or performance issue in an otherwise productive employee. So we tend to accept bad performance or morale, thereby allowing the problem to grow until the pain becomes chronic.

Regarding financial performance, the loss of confidence in the long-term viability of the organization by employees typically brings on one of two responses. In organizations that handle these issues well, employees sometimes rally and become even more committed to the cause. However, in the vast majority of cases, employees who are able to do so leave to find greener pastures. Most employees who leave go without disclosing their actual reasons because of their own tendencies to avoid acute pain.

Boards and administrators are then left with marginal performers, and consequently the value proposition—the basis for the organization's quality claims—is compromised. Said differently and perhaps more clearly, employees are the key to every organization's quality. In a school, it is the teachers and principals who create the value and culture in the organization. Marginal and weak teachers and principals will reduce the perceived quality of the organization, compromising the value proposition. This perceived quality decline will manifest itself in declining enrollment and revenues, and the cascading will continue as turnover is either forced by cost cuts or continues due to these perceived declines—or both.

A certain amount of turnover is, of course, necessary and should be expected. However, turnover should not be explained away when it becomes systemic and statistically significant. Some of my client schools want to survey their employees and the families of their students to learn how they are perceived. While surveys are sometimes valuable, I contend that the families of students vote in favor of the school by re-enrolling their children each year, and teachers and principals indicate that they support the organization by wanting to say on each year.

Turnover is directly linked to financial performance through its cost and its role in the organization's value proposition. Boards and administrators must treat the human resource, including morale and turnover, as part of the organization's financial management strategy. The organization is not only dependent on its employees, but in most cases, the organization's quality is a direct reflection of the quality of its employees. Teachers make the school, create its culture, and carry out its mission. This is true of employees at all nonprofit organizations.

CHAPTER FOUR
The Diagnosis

Beneath the surface of many inquiries I receive from nonprofits is the desire to know how a particular organization compares with its peers. The question is rarely actually asked, but I hear relief in the voice of the nonprofit manager when I begin to complete his sentences and explain that the issues he is facing are common among competitors in other locations. With firms that are discouraged but actually doing relatively well from a financial management standpoint, I try to offer encouragement by explaining their relative position when compared to others in their industry.

An integral part of the financial rescue plan for nonprofits is an assessment of the firm's financial condition. I typically accomplish this through a series of oral questions followed by questions via e-mail and the review of several years of financial information. Bankers and other creditors assess financial strength similarly, although my review is typically deeper from an internal financial management standpoint.

I have created a diagnostic tool in an effort to summarize some of the thought processes I use when assessing the strength of a firm's financial management effort. This diagnostic tool is intended to assist the nonprofit in a self assessment—much like a bank analyzes its clients. The three types—Thriving, Stable, and Declining—are intended to be indicative rather than definitive. There are gaps in various indices, for example, from one type to another, and it is unlikely that any organization will fit perfectly into a particular type. The types are provided so we can determine a best approach for each organization and then, in the context of the organization's financial condition, we can apply each of the financial management tools that will be explained in Part Two.

The Financial Management Diagnostic Tool

	Thriving	Stable	Declining
Liquidity	>150 days of cash	50–149 days of cash	<50 days of cash
Leverage	Debt <50% of assets	Debt <75% of assets	Debt >75% of assets
Solvency	DSC >1.5	DSC >1.0 <1.49	DSC <1.0
Revenue Trend	Stable or growing	Stable to 5% decline	More than 5% decline
Fundraising	>20% of revenue	5–20% of revenue	<5% of revenue
Strategic Plan	Rolling five-year plan	Current year plan only	None or not used
Budget	Perpetual utilization	In place—referenced	None or not used
People Resources	Coaching/feedback	Some coaching	Turnover is high
Banking	Relationship	Transactional	Adversarial
Board Culture	Engaged	Functional	Dysfunctional
Senior Management	Leading	Managing	Supervising

The Thriving organization is able to look further into the future with its planning. Fiscal targets include building endowments, scholarships, reserves, and eventually becoming debt free. Revenue trends are stable, and the organization has found a way to grow at least modestly. Management has the same day-to-day challenges of peers, but has decided to anticipate and prepare for the future. Management often chooses acute pain over chronic pain, and fundraising is an area of focus to meet revenue shortfalls. Board culture is another area of perpetual focus, and the board enjoys transparency and deepening relationships with each other and management. Employees feel valued, and day-to-day management is accomplished such that annual reviews are simply extensions of management's coaching effort. Employees are creative, engaged, and feel a real sense of ownership. Management isn't oppressive, but is focused on leading the organization by planning, organizing, and controlling resources, and providing an environment wherein employees can thrive.

> **DSC: Debt-Service Coverage** is a ratio that examines the amount of cash flow an organization has on hand to make its debt payments. Ideally, this ratio is greater than 1. The ratio is calculated by this formula: Cash Flow divided by Debt Service Requirements for the Same Period.

The Stable organization is able to focus on improving operational management and the building of some cash reserves. Fundraising and debt reduction are long-term goals. The Stable organization aspires to thrive, but its long-term planning isn't effective at present. The firm's liquidity, leverage, and cash flow force the board and management to focus on avoiding financial decline. Management and the board often feel they are doing reasonably well relative to most peers, but they have a sense of treading water or working hard to maintain status quo. Turnover might be a matter of concern, and morale among the staff and other stakeholders isn't at a high level. Management is likely to be technically very capable, but is not really leading the organization proactively into the future with an effective long-term strategic outlook. Threats to survival are not imminent, but the board and management feel they don't have a lot of wiggle room. A downturn in demand, or some other adverse event, could threaten the financial viability of the organization. Management spends a significant amount of time working on operating cash flow, and they aspire to grow to the point where they are able to spend more time working on revenue strategies and thinking and planning for a longer term.

The Declining organization is focused on survival. Debt restructuring and cash flow management are often critical components of the survival plan. Fiscal targets include cutting expenses and increasing revenue from all available sources. Management is distracted from the mission and focused on meeting short-term cash flow requirements. Fiscally, a sense of crisis management is pervasive as management attempts to cut costs. Turnover is typically a challenge in these organizations, and quality initiatives have of necessity taken a back seat to fiscal survival strategies. A cascading of negative events, which may include revenue declines, quality declines, cash flow pressures, turnover among staff and the board, and decline in organizational culture, has occurred, and management and the board are looking for a way to slow the decline so a return to fiscal normalcy is possible. Commitment to the mission is typically strong in these organizations, but organizational failure is likely if a turnaround doesn't occur very soon.

The Rescue Plan

Thriving, Stable, and Declining organizations will approach the elements of the Rescue Plan that follows quite differently. Declining organizations tend to look for operational fixes that will have immediate impact out of necessity. Stable organizations typically look for ways to solidify their position or improve their financial strength. Thriving organizations approach the Rescue Plan as an opportunity to perhaps learn from the best practices of others.

The simplicity of the Rescue Plan will trouble some managers and board members. The tendency of many who find themselves in the Stable to Declining organization types is to react to my simple admonitions with "we have already tried to do that" or "of course we know that." And yet I see so many organizations continuing to decline financially rather than employing the elements of a Rescue Plan. These elements appear simple if taken alone as financial management theory. But the execution of a comprehensive rescue plan and the execution and integration of all the elements can be daunting.

One final word of encouragement: Don't allow yourself to become discouraged based on the relative success of other organizations, and don't believe for a second that success was easy for others. Migrating any organization into the Thriving class requires hard work focused on the critical few elements of a good recovery plan. The tool box that follows is designed to equip your organization to compile its own recovery plan.

The goal of this book and the work I do is not to create perfect organizations that are thriving financially. The goal is to move organizations into a financial position that allows them to focus on the mission well into the future so God is honored. Please see my contact information at the end of the book if I may provide encouragement or assistance to your organization as you implement your recovery plan.

PART TWO
The Financial Rescue Plan

JOHN WARREN

CHAPTER FIVE
The Tool Box

The following chapters are intended to give nonprofit board members, administrators, and senior staff members the tools needed to function successfully in this financially challenging economy. In putting together this Financial Rescue Plan, I rely on my years of banking experience, my knowledge of clients, and my experience in nonprofit financial consulting. This information will also be valuable to parents, volunteers, and others who are invested in schools, churches, ministries, and other nonprofits.

I receive several calls and e-mail contacts per week from nonprofits experiencing financial calamity. While it would be impossible to address the universe of issues that are the subject of all those contacts, my purpose here is to address the common threads so that virtually every organization will benefit from this material.

This book is not intended to replace the good scholarly work that has been done on board governance, financial management, and related subjects. My effort here is to provide a pragmatic guide that will fill some of the gaps and provide clarity to nonprofits that are, like many of my clients, struggling to execute their missions from a financial standpoint.

Organizational management has become underrated as we gravitate toward a culture that values specialization. The commitment required to effectively manage an organization is daunting to many nonprofit professionals and board members. While my client organizations are managed by various types of people with various personality types, I see several common characteristics of effective nonprofit managers:

- Commitment

- Vigilance
- Expertise
- Perpetual personal development
- Attention to detail
- A fastidious approach to measuring results and adjusting accordingly

The subjectivity of these characteristics suits them more appropriately for a book on management theory and psychology. So we can focus on a practical approach to managing nonprofit organizations, in the chapters ahead we'll review key areas of management wherein this managerial skill set is employed. These are the critical functional areas:

- Financial management
- Board management
- Banking relationship management
- Fundraising management
- Risk management
- Marketing management

While specialists in education, health care, social services, and various types of ministry are important components driving an organization's efficacy, management of these functional areas by leaders with big-picture observation and management skills and fastidious attention to detail will distinguish the struggling organizations from those that thrive.

CHAPTER SIX
Financial Management

For our purposes, financial management is the broadest of finance topics for the nonprofit organization. It includes accounting, finance, and all related subjects.

The Difference Between Accounting and Finance

Put simply, accounting keeps score and finance looks more deeply at the reasons behind the accounting data. Further, financial management plans for the future whereas accounting primarily reports the financial implications of the events of the past.

Many of the inquiries I receive from Christian schools, churches, and ministries begin with a description of the history of the organization and a discussion of the financial challenges the organization is facing, or at least the manifestations of those challenges. In most cases, this initial inquiry ends with, "What should we do?" or "What should our financials look like if we want to qualify for a loan?"

Financial management is not as simple as a formula or even a prescription for success. Yes, specific ratios should be used in assessing organizational strength; however, the objective elements of financial management interface with more subjective elements. Successful nonprofits use budgeting, strategic planning, and accounting as tools in their financial management arsenal.

Budgeting

In a well-run organization, the budget and strategic plan are fluid documents that relate to each other and that are adjusted throughout the plan period to ensure that specific, measurable, attainable outcomes are appropriately planned, projected, monitored, and managed. We will examine the budget first, and then the strategic planning process.

For most schools, the fiscal year ends on June 30. For other organizations, a calendar year is often used. Shockingly, some nonprofits employ a "wait and see what happens" approach and don't use a budget at all. Most, however, do develop a budget, and in most organizations the goal is to have the chief financial officer or business manager prepare the budget prior to the beginning of the budgeted period.

The budget is often presented to the board during the last board meeting of the year preceding the budgeted period, and this is typically the first time most board members and even administrators see the budget. Explanations are given for the various income and expense categories such as "enrollment declined from 530 to 517 students; therefore, we are adjusting tuition revenue from X to X minus 13 students' tuition." Or "we struggled to reach our fundraising goals last year with both of our projects, so we're reducing donations by 12 percent this year."

Expenses are often more straightforward. Accountants and bookkeepers compute the precise amount of interest due on loans, the exact amount of salaries and benefits based on teacher contracts and other data, and near-perfect estimates of utilities based on previous years' costs and anticipated rate changes. These very valuable and well-intended employees often glow with glee at the incredibly detailed accuracy of their projections, and they scoff when a board member asks why health insurance premiums are budgeted to increase.

In many cases the budget presentation ends with the discussion of a large deficit and a speech by the superintendent, head of school, or principal about how "we have to trust God again this year to meet our needs and solve our projected operating deficit." While I appreciate the sentiment, and have seen God intervene for organizations in various ways, this budgeting methodology concerns me deeply, as does the theologically weak sentiment expressed to explain the fact that we don't expect to be fiscally solvent this year.

The final chapter of this book will address many of the theological implications of the financial matters addressed herein, but suffice it to say for now that we trust God for **everything**, and He meets our every need. To suggest that we are at the end of our rope and must trustfully rely on God is a biblical sentiment that should permeate our lives. This is the heart of the gospel of Jesus Christ. God loves us, recognizes our sinful state, and sent His son to become sin for us so that we might be cleansed and enjoy restoration to God by faith in Christ. Yes, we desperately depend completely on Him.

However, we can do better than eleventh-hour budgeting done in a vacuum, projecting financial calamity we can't solve. The problem with projecting a deficit and making the "we have to trust God for the difference" statement is twofold.

First, we "have to" trust God for our revenue, our buildings, our health, our salvation, wisdom, tenacity, and our entire lives and being.

Second, projecting a deficit and stating that we have to trust God for the shortfall confirms that we don't have a plan. This budgeting philosophy also says to our constituents that we are projecting failure. If we accomplish all our goals as expressed in our budget, we will fail financially.

Am I suggesting that we don't trust God to meet our needs? Absolutely not. Am I stating that we shouldn't pray for financial solvency? Absolutely not. I'm simply saying that our budget should not predict failure.

Boards and administrators are in leadership positions for a reason. If the first draft of our budget reveals a shortfall, then leadership must employ financial, operational, and strategic management tools to resolve the deficit.

Here is a summary of the perpetual budget process I recommend to my clients:

Step 1: Seek input from the ground up. The Rescue Plan Budgeting Process for Nonprofits starts at the bottom of the organization at least four months prior to the beginning of the budgeted period. In a school, that probably means that principals are asked for capital and operating expense budgets based on anticipated outcomes and needs. Current and even previous years' data should be provided, and a meeting should be held to kick off the process.

Step 2: Senior management analyzes the input provided and develops a working draft. Assumptions are made with respect to revenue changes and significant expense increases and decreases. The first draft of the budget includes an operating budget, a cash flow budget, and a capital budget for replacing or significantly repairing assets such as air conditioning systems. Eventually, all three of these working documents will be completed for monthly use.

Step 3: The budget is presented, with operating, cash flow, and capital elements included, to the board for discussion. Management's assumptions are discussed, as are big-picture items such as tuition price increases, scholarships, fundraising targets, pay increases for teachers, benefit costs, and others. Prior to this point, the external environment would have been reviewed by management, and issues such as competitor pricing and rising health insurance costs would be included in the material discussed. This initial pass at the budget process should ideally occur three months before the beginning of the new fiscal period. The budget is reviewed in the context of the organization's strategic plan, and both the plan and the budget are adjusted so that they do not conflict but work in concert.

Step 4: Staff provides additional data and makes changes to the draft budget based on board input. Management discusses these changes, evaluates all data, revisits the entire budget, and formulates a new draft. Difficult decisions such as tuition increases, staff reductions, fundraising changes, and other operating expense savings are baked into the budget at this point based on board and management input. The goal throughout the process is to be realistic, transparent, and as accurate as possible.

Inevitably, in a school environment in particular, fundraising will be the number that is plugged into the budget based on the remaining need after all other changes are made. This number also must be tested so it will be realistic. Simply plugging this number into the budget without regard for the likelihood of its attainment will probably result in the failure to address other budget categories that should be adjusted.

Step 5: Management presents the budget to the board for the second time, with adjustments made pursuant to the previous discussions and input provided. Note that the board's finance committee might accomplish some of these steps ahead of time by consulting with management, but the full board should be involved in the review process that begins with Step 3 above. This presentation should occur at least two months prior to the budgeted period. Board input is again sought, and the budget is reviewed in the context of the strategic plan.

At this stage, discussion should focus on pivotal budget items such as revenue, key expenses, capital expenses, and cash-flow shortfalls. Peripheral items, such as small-expense line items, should have been resolved by management prior to this presentation to the board. The critical few but significant items should be the focus of this discussion. The senior manager of the organization should lead the discussion, working hard to focus board members on these critical few items when they naturally tend to opt for discussing easier, smaller issues in the budget.

Step 6: The board approves the budget. If this is not accomplished in Step 5 above, any changes caused as a result of Step 5 are incorporated into the budget, and an additional meeting is held within two weeks of Step 5 to approve the final operating, capital, and cash-flow budgets. See Chapter Six for the importance of unanimity and commitment at this stage of the budget process.

Step 7: At the board meeting preceding the beginning of the budgeted period, the final budget and all supporting documentation (performance plans, monitoring reports, and departmental breakdowns) are presented to the board. The board and management lock arms at this point and commit to the achievement of this budget and the accompanying strategies and goals that are inherent in its assumptions.

Step 8: The budget becomes an integral part of the monthly financial reporting process. Actual versus budget performance is tracked, and this tracking is pushed down to the lowest possible level. Budget data are also used in performance management for those employees who are department heads with actual budgeted outcomes.

Step 9: Management and the board work throughout the budgeted year to tweak the budget when appropriate. This tweaking is not a means of resolving shortfalls, but it does reflect external and internal environmental changes that weren't contemplated as part of the original budget assumptions. For example, if fundraising lags behind the monthly budgeted amount, we don't simply revise the number downward. We adjust our strategies so that we accomplish our goals. On the other hand, if enrollment dropped 10 percent at the last minute prior to the beginning of the school year, the appropriate revenue and corresponding expense adjustments should be made by management and reported to and approved by the board.

Step 10: The strategic plan is perpetually evaluated in the context of actual performance. The organization's performance relative to budget is a great jumping-off place for this evaluation.

Strategic Planning

Much has been written about strategic planning. Strategic Planning 101 includes many elements, including the following:

- A mission statement
- SWOT analysis
- Goals
- Strategies

- Tactics supporting those strategies
- Various measurement processes

But for our purposes, I am focused on the practical elements of an effective strategic planning process and resultant document. We want to avoid the weeds and trees and focus on the forest. My goal is to give you a view of strategic planning that alters the process from frightening to understandable and the document from large, clumsy, and collecting dust on the bookshelves of a few employees, to an efficient, straightforward guide used throughout all levels of the organization perpetually.

Much is made of mission statements by those who claim to be strategic planning experts. While a clear understanding of the organization's mission is important for the board, management, staff, and everyone involved, the actual mission statement should be simple and easy to understand. It is not necessary or desirable to use a thesaurus when crafting a mission statement. And although the mission statement is typically printed on the first page of the strategic plan, its formation is not the first step in the process.

The first step in planning is to clearly understand the current situation. Most organizations are able to assess and understand financial issues, and a number of these tools will be valuable to the strategic planner. It is imperative that we know who we are, what we do, and where we stand.

The analysis typically begins with a SWOT analysis, which calls for examining organizational strengths, weaknesses, opportunities, and threats both internally and externally.

First, data must be collected. The Census Bureau and groups such as the Association of Christian Schools International and other organizations with specific industry expertise and data can be valuable resources for external data. Accrediting bodies and governmental entities can also provide external data.

Internal data will come from your accounting systems and senior managers. Note that I didn't prescribe the composition of a planning committee. That's because the entire company should be involved in the process. The senior-most manager should lead the process, and most organizations prefer to form a committee consisting of a few board members and senior managers. However, the entire organization should participate.

Agreeing on the organization's basic internal and external strengths, weaknesses, opportunities, and threats is often the most challenging part of the process. Remember to constantly test ideas for materiality or whether or not they are pivotal. A leaky pipe in a bathroom is not a strategic planning threat, and the tensile strength of the paper clips is not a strength.

The most challenging aspect of this phase is pulling back the camera enough to ensure that the strengths and weaknesses of the organization, from both internal and external perspectives, are captured thoroughly without including minutia. This balance is difficult to achieve.

A SWOT analysis is time consuming. It should also be revisited as needed throughout the other steps in the planning process.

The second step is to establish goals. Thus far, we have focused on who we are, where we are, and the opportunities and threats we face. Next we focus on where we want to go in the context of our mission and our SWOT analysis. Goals should be clearly articulated, avoiding nebulous adjectives such as "best, strongest, most impactful, most visible" and the like. Appropriate goals for a school might include the following:

- Grow enrollment from 572 students to 650 students by the end of fiscal year 2015–2016.

- Improve ACT score averages from a composite 25 to 28 by the end of a future fiscal year.

- Increase fundraising from $50,000 to $250,000 during the plan year.

- Improve staff retention from X percent to Y percent during the plan year.

- Balance the cash flow operating statement annually.

- Improve retention of students in transitional years, grades five to six and eight to nine, from current levels of 72 percent and 68 percent, respectively, to 85 percent and 90 percent.

The strategic goals for a school would not include:

- Serve our community better.

- Improve our image in the community.

- Develop happier families.

- Do better in terms of our employees' satisfaction.

Serving, improving, developing, and doing better are admirable concepts, but they aren't meaningful goals for strategic planning purposes. **One exception I would make for the Christian organization would be the biblical mandate that we honor God with all that we do, or that we encourage students, faculty, and staff to follow Christ with all that we do.** Christian organizations should include this mandate in their strategic plan, and this concept should permeate their culture.

The third step in the planning process is the development of a handful (five to ten) strategies the organization should focus on to accomplish its goals in the context of its SWOT factors. If necessary, the planners can state the mission prior to this stage. Most schools and other organizations have articulated their mission previously, and a more thorough assessment of the mission might be necessary. But for now, a simple statement of mission is adequate.

Writers of scholarly works on strategic planning often say goals must be SMART: Specific, Measurable, Attainable, Realistic, and Timely. While this acronym is somewhat juvenile and contains some redundancy, it provides an adequate guide for strategy development and statement. These strategies continue to build the strategic planning skeletal structure that has been started by the SWOT analysis and stated goals of the organization. Each goal should have several strategies (three to five on average) that will result in the attainment of the goal. Some strategies will help accomplish more than one goal. As such, the strategy should be repeated throughout the document in each appropriate goal section.

A strategy to improve culture and organizational communication, for instance, might affect the goal of retaining both staff and students. A strategy to improve curriculum might raise ACT scores as well as boosting teacher satisfaction and retention.

Strategies will, by definition, be more loosely defined than step four of the process, the development of specific tactics. Tactics are specific steps that will be taken to accomplish the strategies, which accomplish goals. Here's an example:

Goal: Improve student retention in certain grades.

Strategy: Communicate more effectively throughout the organization.

Tactic: Send newsletters to fifth- and eighth-grade parents every six weeks throughout the school year, focusing on the strengths of the middle and high schools.

Another example might be a goal of being debt free by a certain date. Strategies might include the paying for all expansion with cash raised through contributions. One tactic might be to target specific fundraising projects to meet expansion needs. Another might be to conduct a fundraising campaign. Yet another might be to build a contingency fund to avoid borrowing to fund unexpected capital maintenance items. Yet another tactic might be the use of excess operating cash flow to retire debt by using a faster-than-required repayment schedule.

The importance of the strategic plan relates as much to its utilization as its formation. The best-developed strategic planning document is not valuable if it isn't used. The plan should be reviewed perpetually, and board meetings should include the plan as an agenda item for almost every meeting. The plan should be the basis for budgeting, for performance standards and reviews, and for board and management action of various types. The plan should be tweaked as needed, and both the budget and the strategic plan should guide the board and management as they make policy and management decisions, respectively.

The goals of various departments and functions within the organization should be established so they are reflected in the performance reviews of the individuals in these departments and roles. It follows that if the individuals are accomplishing their performance goals, then the organization is accomplishing its stated strategic and budgetary goals. For those inclined to obsess over minutia, this doesn't mean that we carve up all the income and expenses and assign every dollar to an individual. However, we generally want to coordinate the organization's goals with departmental or cost-center budgets and individual performance goals so they work in concert.

If we have departments or individuals whose goals don't fit with our strategic plan, we either have departments or individuals who are not necessary to the organization or a strategic plan that isn't thorough. Tangential or support departments are sometimes necessary but difficult to tie directly to the strategic plan. Nevertheless, with some effort even these tangential areas can be included in the plan. As painful as the process can be, organizations must analyze all departments and people in terms of efficacy and necessity. Our tendency to avoid acute pain makes the process difficult, but acute pain is often needed to improve organizational efficiency.

The following is a simple outline of a goal and the accompanying strategies and tactics sections of a strategic plan for a nonprofit organization.

Goal: Increase revenue by 4 percent in fiscal 2015, three percent in 2016, and three percent in 2017.

Strategy: Raise tuition and fundraising revenue each year of the plan period.

Tactic—Increase tuition by two percent for each year of the plan period.

Tactic—Conduct fundraising campaign in 2015 with pledges for three years.

Tactic—Rewrite scholarship and financial aid policies during 2015.

Strategy: Grow enrollment by 15 students each in fiscal 2015, 2016, and 2017.

Tactic—Conduct open house meetings for prospective families monthly.

Tactic—Restructure website by January 1 with improved marketing to prospective families.

Tactic—Hold superintendent breakfast meetings with current families weekly to determine improvements needed to our communication and marketing strategies, meeting with all school families every fiscal year.

Tactic—Admissions director to contact the two area K-8 schools during each school year, building a database that will allow marketing for high school admission by graduating eighth graders. The effort is to partner with these schools for referral of seventh and eighth grade families. A quid pro quo might be the use of our athletic fields and auditorium by these schools at no cost.

The Accounting Function

Every nonprofit organization should have an effective strategic plan, annual and monthly budgets, and annual accounting statements prepared according to generally accepted accounting principles. These statements should be prepared internally unless no staff member has the expertise to do so. In those cases, the certified public accountant (CPA) who does the annual review or audit should set up a system so a bookkeeper can perform data input and monthly financials can be efficiently prepared.

Whether the organization performs an annual review or audit depends on the amount of debt and requirements of creditors, as well as the size of the organization. A review should be sufficient in most cases; however, a third-party examination of internal controls and a sampling of asset and liability accuracy, which are elements of an audit, can be valuable. Having said that, CPA recommendations about controls can be difficult for small nonprofits to implement; thus, leaders must exercise judgment regarding the value of the recommendations versus their costs.

Whether a review or audit is prepared annually, it is important that it be done on time. Warning signs creditors look for include delays in financial statement preparation and changing CPA firms. At times, delays are inevitable and changes are warranted. But recognize that creditors will be troubled by these events. Proactively explain to creditors that these events are occurring and explain the reasons for them.

The internal accounting function encompasses several tasks, including these:

- Bank statement reconciliation
- Accounts receivable management
- Accounts payable management
- General ledger management
- Preparation of monthly financial statements

Financials should be produced on a timely basis, and board meetings should be scheduled so financials aren't outdated. Financials should be sufficiently detailed, but it isn't necessary to include every general ledger subaccount in the financial statements. Statements should be presented in a clear format. Various types of comparative data may be helpful:

- Current period
- Year-to-date
- Previous month
- Same month last year
- Last year's year-to-date
- Current budget

Importantly, these spreadsheets must be organized and adequately explained at all board meetings. Generally accepted accounting principles should be followed, and that means accruals are accurate and not manipulated to conceal adverse information.

If your organization lacks the internal expertise to offer an adequate overview of financial performance to your board, please retain a company like mine for these purposes. At relatively low cost, an experienced person can bring financials to life, allowing a board to understand the relationships among the various statements and periods observed.

The efficacy of the internal financial reporting function is critical to the early identification of issues that should concern management and the board. A large percentage of my clients either don't understand their own financial statements, don't communicate them clearly to their board, or even deliberately conceal actual financial results from their board. This is tantamount to malpractice or fraud, and should not be tolerated by any nonprofit administrator...period.

Knowing that we have problems is essential to solving them. Board members should look for warning signs. For example, if the income statement and balance sheet don't reveal distress, but payables aren't paid on time or other cash flow issues are evident, additional questions should be asked. It is appropriate for a manager or board member to ask questions when warning signs, concerns, or ambiguity appear. It is inappropriate for managers and board members to deliberately attempt to discredit each other with ambush attacks with respect to financial performance. Judgment is required when deciding when and where to ask pointed questions about financial performance; however, I have a bias toward having these discussions with the entire board present so the answers are heard firsthand by all stakeholders.

A few of my clients' reluctance to report financial data clearly has caused challenges to worsen as issues have gone unaddressed. Concealment is not appropriate, and the thorough and accurate reporting of financial status and performance are critical. Clients who deliberately color their financial condition are organizations I cannot work with because of the difficulty involved in assessing financial condition. Further, it is inconsistent with the character of an organization that calls itself Christian for the organization to misrepresent its financial condition. Our theology and our business practices should not be in conflict. There is no principle of greater good that would warrant deception of any kind.

The Numbers Tell a Story

A nonprofit's financial statements tell a story and should be contrasted with expectations and the strategic plan. A seasoned financial officer can explain the story behind the numbers in the context of the SWOT analysis and goals delineated in the budget and strategic plan.

The balance sheet is a snapshot of assets and obligations, while the income statement tells the operating story over a period of time. Our cash flow, which is driven by the data from these statements, indicates our ability to meet current obligations. Obligations come in the form of operating expenses, capital expenditures, and debt payments. Board discussions on financial statements should reflect these relationships.

The presenter of financial data should tell the board and management the story the financials reveal. Simply reciting the data is not adequate. Board members should receive financials a few days in advance of meetings so that review of the data isn't rushed and questions may be formulated. Board members shouldn't share the data outside of the board, and questions should be held until board meetings so all stakeholders directly hear the question and answer.

Budget exceptions should be highlighted and thoroughly explained. Deviations from budget that are known by the finance department or management should be proactively explained so strategies and budgets may be adjusted. Adjusting budgets so the organization meets budgeted expectations is a foolish exercise, but adjusting budgets to reflect a material change in a financial reality is prudent. For example, if we missed our enrollment projections by a significant amount, it makes sense to flex our budget to reflect the change. If our landlord doubled the rent during a budget period, it makes sense to adjust that budget category. If, on the other hand, we overspent on supplies, we wouldn't adjust the budget but would note the deviation and would correct the overspending going forward. As with most elements of financial management, these require deft discernment and thoughtful communication and execution.

Ratio Analysis

In addition to the elements presented above, the accounting and finance presentation should include ratio analysis. Financial institutions and creditors of all types use financial analysis to determine the creditworthiness of any organization. Here, we'll focus on general ratio and other financial analyses. Chapter Seven, "Banking Relationship Management," will address financial institutions' use of ratio analysis in credit decisions. Here, we will discuss ratio analysis for internal management purposes.

> **Ratio analysis:** A set of calculations comparing the relative strengths of items in an organization's financial statements, typically focusing on liquidity, leverage, and solvency.

The most elementary type of financial analysis is trend analysis. Trend analysis views changes in the income statement and balance sheet over time, and uses the data to develop valuable management information about possible trends.

Another basic type of analysis is common sizing analysis. This type views various income statement and balance sheet categories as a percentage of the total for the category. For example, it might be valuable to know that 20 percent of our revenue came from fundraising last year, but we have fallen to 10 percent this year. The obvious weaknesses in this form of analysis include relevance and the fact that both the numerator and denominator might be moving to create the change. For example, if our contributions decreased from 20 percent to 10 percent of our total revenue, and our enrollment improved dramatically during the same period, we might find that contributions didn't decline in absolute terms.

Discussions of this type of analysis must be led with sound judgment and with a focus on valuable strategic and operating implications of the data. In our example above, we might conclude that donations should have increased on a level commensurate with revenue increases due to our enrollment increases, or we might conclude that contributions from newly enrolled families tend to lag by some time period because they require assimilation into the culture before becoming part of the fundraising base.

Ratio analysis typically focuses on liquidity, leverage, and solvency. I will summarize a few ratios for illustrative purposes, but ratio analysis is really only valuable to the extent that it provides useful data for financial management.

Current ratio is calculated by this formula: Current Assets divided by Current Liabilities. This ratio indicates the company's ability to meet current obligations with its liquid assets.

Debt ratio, or debt-to-worth ratio, is calculated this way: Total Debt divided by Net Worth (or Fund Balance). This ratio addresses long-term solvency and general financial strength. It reveals the company's leverage, and while it can be argued that leverage can make an organization more efficient from a financial standpoint, a lower debt ratio is generally preferred. One way to view the debt ratio is to consider it in the context of how much of the company is owned or controlled by the company (equity) versus the amount that is controlled by outsiders (debt).

Debt service coverage ratio is calculated by this general formula: Cash Flow for the Period divided by Cash Required to Service Debt. This ratio indicates short-term solvency, and it is predictive of cash operating performance. Third parties typically set a standard of at least 1.25 times for this indicator, and top-performing companies typically enjoy debt service coverage ratios of 1.5 or higher.

Days payable and days receivable are also useful calculations that reflect the average days outstanding for payables and receivables. These ratios reveal the source of cash flow issues.

Dashboard reports that summarize the financial performance of the organization should be constructed for internal management purposes. The reports should be understandable, and they should contain the general financial data needed by management for day-to-day decision-making purposes. A similar report that summarizes financial performance on one or two pages is usually helpful to nonprofit board members. This summary report should be the focal point of the financial report at board meetings, but it isn't a substitute for detailed statements, which should also be included in the board package each month.

CHAPTER SEVEN
Board Management

An organization's chief executive, as well as the board itself, play a role in board management. A board should self-police and self-manage to ensure that it is playing its role fully without taking on a larger role than is prudent. Much has been written on this topic, but let's avoid discussion of a particular governance model and focus on big-picture concepts and practical guidance.

The Rescue Plan Theory of Organizational Dysfunction

Groups of people sometimes behave badly. A group will engage in denial and will act in a manner inconsistent with the morality and intellectual ability of the average individual in the group. This "dumbing down" will occur naturally if not countered by group leadership and culture. Further, culture in a group setting will decline naturally. Maintaining healthy elements of culture—or improving culture—requires leadership and a level of commitment in which most people and organizations are not prepared to engage.

My client base includes organizations with boards of various types and sizes. Some of the boards have staggered member terms, and others have perpetual terms so that members serve until they resign or are asked to leave. Board sizes range from just three or four members to twelve or more, and the average board has about eight members. Schools and other organizations sometimes employ advisory boards if they are affiliated with or owned by a church. Most schools and ministries have their own nonprofit corporation and a board that is entirely separate from any affiliated organization.

Schools are sometimes run by or owned by the parents of current students. In other cases, an association effectively owns the school, and the association consists of current families, alumni, and other affiliated parties. Still other schools are managed solely by the board. These configurations are outside of the scope of this book, but in my opinion, a separate 501(c)(3) entity with a governing board is essential for the successful management of a nonprofit organization. Advisory boards and church-owned schools with token boards are formulas for confusion unless clear accountability and roles are established. I have several client organizations at which a change occurred in the controlling church which then compromised the financial integrity of the school.

Very few nonprofit companies are aware of the prescribed structure, governance, and management roles in their articles of incorporation or bylaws. These documents are important, but I find that they are rarely read until there is a disagreement or crisis. These documents should be examined and referenced routinely as the board conducts its business and the administration executes its duties. These documents should be clearly understood and modified, if needed, proactively rather than reactively to ensure they reflect the organization's culture and goals in terms of the way the board and management must conduct business.

Many nonprofit organizations do not follow their governing documents' prescriptions for handling corporate matters. While some are aware that the provisions in these documents aren't followed, others simply don't look at them at all.

I favor a model of governance wherein all board members are equal in authority and accountability, and all have one vote. I favor a structure in that weightier matters which alter the organization's board composition or executive management require a supermajority vote of two-thirds of the board. An organization might even have certain matters of policy and strategy that require a unanimous vote. If that is the case, the emotional and mental status of board candidates should be carefully reviewed, as one member would be able to create gridlock on a potentially important issue such as a merger or modification of the composition of the board itself.

Staggered terms are probably prudent in some cases, but consider five-year over three-year terms so board continuity is assured. With staggered terms, board members' terms expire at various times, so wholesale board changes don't occur at once. However, this might limit the board's ability to add talented members as they become available, and it might limit the term of a talented board member who could otherwise serve effectively for a longer term.

I have seen articles of incorporation that prescribe multiple classes of voting board members wherein a select group of board members serve permanent terms and have stronger voting rights, and others are elected for short terms and have limited voting rights. While this might work for some organizations, it can create confusion and divisions on the board based on perceived class or caliber.

I favor indefinite board service by board members, with specific voting requirements and criteria for removal. I also favor a review process that includes a background check for new board members along with a supermajority vote requirement for admission to the board after an introduction and period of due diligence.

What Does a Board Actually Accomplish?

The most effective boards set policy and big-picture strategy, and the only official reporting relationship in place is between the board and the chief executive. All other employees report either directly to the chief executive or to senior managers who report to the chief executive.

A board does not manage the day-to-day operations of the organization, but the chief executive might seek counsel from the board on such matters. The board should discipline itself to avoid reaching into the minutia and to focus instead on setting and reviewing policy and strategy.

The chief executive and chief financial officer are typically the only two internal employees who report to the board as a routine part of every board meeting. Various department heads might do so when invited due to an agenda item requiring their expertise.

My experience affirms that voting board members and only as many others as necessary from the organization should be present at each board meeting so discussion is free and open without regard for interpretation issues and other sensitivities. Exceptions, of course, may be made for senior executives whose role dictates greater board involvement; however, if a significant number of non-board employees are presenting at each board meeting, then each board meeting agenda should include an executive session, in which only the directors and chief executive are present for additional discussion.

The following is a list of my best board practices and procedures.

Board meetings should be held in the morning or at lunch or early afternoon if possible. Evening board meetings can be tiring, and important business might not receive the appropriate level of attention and energy. This will prove challenging for some directors given their other priorities; however, my experience is that directors can make the necessary changes in their schedules to accommodate earlier meeting times. As a courtesy to directors, board meetings for the entire year should be scheduled and notices issued prior to the beginning of the year.

Board meetings should be attended in person, and board members should not miss more than two meetings per year. Board meetings should be held monthly and more often as needed. Board meetings may be held by phone with all board members on a secured conference line in cases when physical attendance is impossible, but phone polling to vote on board issues—when board members are called one at a time by the chairman or designee—is not prudent under any circumstances. The obvious reason for this is the fact that each board member should hear the entire discussion on the subject rather than relying on one member to relay thoughts to each member privately.

Board meetings should be efficient. Meetings should last about one to two hours, except in cases wherein weightier topics require more time, and should start on time. They should be efficiently run pursuant to a modified version of *Robert's Rules of Order*, with motions being made and appropriately seconded followed by voice votes and hand votes when necessary to achieve an accurate count. Further discussion should be allowed, but only after the motion and second. Careful notes should be taken by the board secretary reflecting the motion made, the party making the motion and second, and the outcome of the vote, along with any abstentions or negative votes.

Conflicts of interest should be avoided. Generally speaking, a conflict of interest occurs when the personal or business interests of a board member could potentially conflict with the interests of the organization. Members with conflicts should not only abstain from voting but should leave the room during discussion and voting unless the conflicted member is asked to provide information for consideration by the board. For example, if a contractor is a board member, and his firm is one of four bidding on replacement of a driveway at the school, this board member should not be present for discussion or voting on the subject, and his or her bid should be reviewed similarly to other bids. Common sense and taking great care to avoid a conflict of interest or the appearance of a conflict should be exercised by all in these matters.

Conversations should remain in the meeting. Discussions about official board business should not occur outside of board meetings, either among directors or with staff, unless the purpose of the contact is to collect information from a staff member at the direction of the chief executive or board. In other words, if board members attend the same church and happen to spend time on Sunday in a discussion at the church, official school business should not be discussed.

Detailed minutes should be kept. Board minutes are presented in draft form at the following meeting. The draft should then be reviewed and approved for insertion into the official record at the following meeting. Corrections should be made in the form of a motion to approve the minutes: "I move to approve the minutes of the last meeting with the following change." The bylaws and articles of the organization should be followed at all times, but in the absence of clear direction to the contrary in these documents, sensitive issues should be included in the minutes by reference only. A good rule of thumb in determining whether or not an item is included in the minutes is to assume the minutes will be read in a court of law in a situation wherein the board is defending the action taken. Thus, a sufficient level of detail should be included without including superfluous or even inflammatory information. Another healthy assumption is to view the minutes in the context of their being used for a review in five years. Does the detail tell the story with clarity? Could a third party read and understand the action taken? Does the action taken appear, solely from a read of the minutes, to have received the appropriate level of care by the board?

Board members should develop a collegial culture. Nevertheless, the culture should be one in which opposing views are welcomed and thoroughly vetted. Opposing views shouldn't be treated as personal attacks, and freedom to think and speak should predominate. Opposing views should be voiced in the meetings only, and a spirit of collegial cooperation should prevail.

The entire board approves all successful actions even when dissenting votes are cast. By this I mean that the entire board is to support all board action taken, even board members who cast dissenting votes. This avoids comments like "I tried to tell them" or "I voted no and knew this wouldn't work," along with other prideful, destructive claims. If a motion passes, it passes for the entire organization, and it is the duty of every board member to lock arms and support the action regardless of the level of debate over the matter in the privacy of the board meeting.

Final thoughts on board practices:

Board meetings should be held in a professional setting. A good boardroom is comfortable, and confidential information may be discussed there without concerns about compromise. Cell phones should not be visible and should be silenced, and the entire board should give the appropriate level of care to the entire meeting. The agenda should be distributed in advance, according to the requirements of the articles or bylaws. Appropriate advance notice should be given for ad hoc board meetings. Board meetings should not be recorded electronically, and all board documents and board packages that are not official documents for preservation should be left at the meeting and shredded by the chief executive.

CHAPTER EIGHT
Banking Relationship Management

It is necessary for every nonprofit organization to understand that your banking relationship is to be managed by you. While the subject isn't terribly broad, I'm going to provide you with some practical thoughts for managing your banking relationship.

The Rescue Plan Theory of Bank Relationship Management

Your banker is not your friend. She is the provider of a commodity and related services. Multiple banking relationships are in order for every nonprofit.

First, develop and maintain a relationship with at least two and preferably three banks. You might want to use one for an operating checking account with a money market account for excess cash, another for reserve funds or endowment funds, and a third for payroll or some other aspect of your finances.

At least two of your banks should be small community or small regional banks. Pull a report on the bank from the FDIC (See sidebar), and have your chief financial officer review the bank's financial performance to ensure your bank is reasonably financially healthy. You might also want to discuss FDIC insurance limits with your bank to ensure that your deposits are protected by the government. Each account can only be insured up to a certain amount, so this process might require opening accounts at additional banks, and your bank might offer tools that allow you to insure a greater share of your deposits.

What a UBPR Is and How to Get One

The Federal Financial Institutions Examination Council, a division of the Federal Deposit Insurance Corporation, stores financial information for most institutions insured by the FDIC. To find out about your bank, or a bank you're considering for a new relationship, pull a UBPR—a Uniform Bank Performance Report. This document summarizes the bank's condition, including its earnings, balance sheet, liquidity, and capital.

Go to http://www.ffiec.gov/UBPR.htm and click on "UBPR Reports." On the next page, choose "Uniform Bank Performance Report" from the pull-down menu and put in the bank's name. Click "Search," then choose a reporting period and click "Generate Report." You'll need to have your popup blocker turned off.

If your organization already has bank debt, I encourage you to conduct your depository banking at a separate bank unless your loan agreement requires that you keep deposit accounts there. "Right of offset" rules allow a bank to seize deposited funds under the same tax identification number as a loan in default under certain circumstances. But the bank can only do this with its own accounts. In other words, if your checking account and your mortgage are with the same bank and you miss your mortgage payment, the bank can take the money out of your checking account to cover the mortgage. But Bank A can't go to Bank B and seize your deposits to cover a missed loan payment at Bank A— unless a court action allows it to. Under certain loan agreement provisions, your bank can declare default for any number of technical reasons related to timely payment or covenant compliance, and they may accelerate the entire balance of the loan and seize all the organization's cash held in that bank. The timing of this seizure can be crippling to your organization, as it can occur without notice.

Here are several practical guidelines for maintaining healthy banking relationships.

Befriend several bankers. Meet finance professionals through your school or organization's family, your church, civic organizations, or country club. Bankers who are currently at middle management levels might be a valuable resource to you in the future.

Get to know your loan officer if you have a bank loan of any sort. Invite the loan officer to get to know the chief executive of your organization. Provide a tour of your facilities and provide other organizational exposure to your banker.

Provide all required information to your banker on time—including payments. If for any reason this becomes impossible, communicate proactively with your banker. Explain the reason for the late payment or information delay, promise to remedy the matter by a certain date, and promise to follow up by phone or in person. Generally speaking, bankers respond well to proactive client communication, even when the news is bad. Explain changes in your financial position and let your banker know you are running your organization proactively.

Get to know several levels of bankers at all the banks with which you do business. Let them get to know your company and its culture.

Don't make presumptions. You can't expect the bankers who serve your board members' companies to be as warm to serving your school or organization. Well-meaning board members often introduce their bankers to your school because they believe they can transfer their personal goodwill into a banking relationship for your school. This is rarely the case.

Maintain at least two and preferably three or more banking relationships. If your organization is burdened by heavy debt, dividing the debt, when possible, among two or more banks makes sense. Bank cultures change and banks fail. For these and other reasons, banks' appetites for credit change over time. It makes sense to have a competitive environment in which multiple relationships allow you to get multiple quotes on new loan terms and on renewals. Starting from scratch and searching for a new bank is much more difficult than expanding a relationship with an existing bank.

Top officers should know bankers. The chief executive in the organization and the CFO should meet multiple bankers at various levels at each of your organization's banks. It is important for the banker to know the senior-most executive in the company, as well as the most competent accounting person. The two people in these roles, along with one or two other key people in some cases, will give the banker comfort with the quality of management and the integrity of the company's financial data. These subjective matters should not be underestimated when managing the company's banking relationship.

Look for external funding sources. Options such as tax exempt bond financing and private equity might be available. These funding vehicles for real estate debt can have very attractive terms, and these alternatives should be explored with a professional financial advisor. Be aware of predators and advisors with less credibility, as they can have agendas that include acquiring your real estate while pretending to help you in the short run.

Tax-Exempt Bond Financing

Tax-exempt bond financing is a broad topic, and its ambiguity causes a lot of misinformation and missed opportunity. There are a number of types of tax-exempt bond financing arrangements. For our purposes we will exclude "church bonds," which are sold to a group of constituents by a consultant representing a church or other organization for the purposes of funding growth or retiring debt.

Tax-exempt bond financing includes those financing vehicles that allow the lender or investor to earn tax-exempt interest. The attraction of this to the nonprofit is that typically the terms will be more favorable than those offered through taxable financial vehicles. This is not always the case, but the theory is the basis for using these instruments.

Tax-exempt bond issues can be structured in a variety of ways. For our discussion, let's focus on the three most common types. In all three, a qualifying nonprofit organization borrows money from the bondholder, or investor, at a fixed or floating interest rate, much like a typical real estate loan.

With tax-exempt bond financing, there are typically a few additional moving parts. These might include a trustee, who is responsible for administering the bond issue requirements, collecting and distributing payments, and overseeing compliance with terms and conditions; a bond counsel, an attorney who is well versed in structuring tax-exempt financing; bond holders, the parties who are actually investing in or making the loan; a governmental entity with the authority to issue bonds; and a bank, which might provide credit enhancements and other financing instruments.

Here are the three most common types of bonds used by my clients:

- Direct bank debt, which is done in the form of a tax-exempt bond
- A traditional bond issue with a credit enhancement provided by a bank
- A direct bond issue without a credit enhancement of any kind

Let's discuss each in turn.

Direct Bank Debt

This type of tax-exempt bond looks and feels like a traditional bank loan with some additions. The bank seeks approval from a taxing authority such as a municipality, and the bank typically has a wholly owned entity that serves as trustee. The bank's wholly owned capital markets group might serve as trustee, thereby administering the bond issue. The bank makes the loan, and the interest is treated as tax exempt by the bank's accountants. This is attractive to the bank because tax-exempt interest income means the yield on the loan is higher. This can be attractive to the borrower because the bank might pass on some of the tax savings through a lower interest rate on the loan.

The qualifying process and terms for this type of financing are similar if not identical to a traditional bank loan. Smaller banks not earning predictable profits will not typically engage in this type of financing, and larger banks don't tend to favor it because of the additional variables involved with all the steps and parties in the process. This type of financing also typically means higher closing costs for the borrower. Consequently, the number of direct bank loans structured as tax-exempt bond issues has diminished in recent years.

Traditional Bond Issue with Credit Enhancement

If your organization is financially strong enough to qualify for a bank loan, but not strong enough to prompt institutional investors to buy bonds as part of your financing package, then you might consider asking a bank to provide a credit enhancement, such as a letter of credit. This commits the bank to fund its face amount in the event of certain trigger events. Those events typically relate to timely payment, covenant compliance, and general financial strength.

Bond purchasers in these transactions can rely on the strength of the bank rather than that of the nonprofit. These letters of credit promise to pay off the bond holders if the borrower defaults on their obligation; therefore, the bonds receive the rating of the bank and are typically placed in a low-risk portfolio by the investor. The bond issue receives the rating of the large bank involved, investors rely on the strength of that bank as support for the soundness of their investment, and the nonprofit receives the proceeds, much like a traditional loan or direct bank debt.

The costs of this type of transaction typically include those of a direct bank loan or bond issue, plus the cost of the letter of credit. Letters of credit typically require an annual fee of 1 to 2 percent per year. This is quite costly, and the uncertainty of annual approval by the bank makes this type of financing less than ideal for the typical nonprofit entity.

Several years ago, a client of mine engaged a large bank to meet their financing needs. At that time, to protect themselves from rising interest rates, they not only sought bond financing with a letter of credit, they also purchased an instrument known as an interest rate swap. That effectively gave the borrower a fixed interest rate on the debt while providing the lender, or bondholders, with a floating rate. The organization paid a handsome premium for the interest rate swap and significant closing costs on the bond issue. Over time, the bank became concerned about the financial condition of the borrower and began increasing the annual fee on the letter of credit. Incredibly, the bank that sold the nonprofit the interest rate swap to fix the organization's interest rate effectively increased the cost of financing each year by raising the letter of credit fee from 1 percent to 1.25 percent to 1.50 percent to 1.75 percent.

My point in sharing this story is that exposure to annual approval and pricing on a credit enhancement, such as a letter of credit, can create as much vulnerability as short-term maturities and variable interest rates on the underlying credit facility. Don't fall for the illusion that your organization's debt obligations are fixed if a credit enhancement with an annual maturity is in place to support the obligations. This particular story had a happy ending, with the refinancing of all the firm's debts with the third type of tax-exempt bond outlined below.

Direct Bond Issue

This type of bond involves bond counsel, a bond underwriter, a trustee, and bondholders (similar to the second type above), but a credit enhancement is not required and a bank is not involved. This type of financing is only available to a creditworthy organization that would typically qualify for traditional financing. In this environment, however, we find that banks are looking to exit relationships with 501(c)(3) organizations, and generally speaking they are not looking to make new loans to such entities.

The direct bond issue can be attractive in these cases. The bond underwriter reviews financial data, much like the review done by a bank but a bit more pragmatically, and determines that the institutional investors—think mutual funds, investment firms, and other groups of individual investors—are likely to buy the bonds. Underwriting material is prepared, the investors agree to purchase the bonds, and a governmental entity approves the bond issue in their name.

Bond counsel prepares all the documents throughout the process, a closing occurs, and proceeds are disbursed. The primary advantages to this type of bond are the absence of any sort of credit enhancement or other bank involvement that would require short-term modifications, and the fact that a long-term interest rate and payment schedule can be put in place for the right borrower. Several of our clients' bonds have had twenty- to twenty-five-year terms with fixed interest rates for the full term.

Among my most challenging conversations are those with clients who have been victims of a bad banking relationship, when I attempt to explain that a market exists for them that will provide long loan terms with fixed rates. The conversation usually includes the CFO saying, "Are you telling me we can have a 6 percent fixed rate for twenty-five years with no short-term rate modification or maturity?" It gives me pleasure to answer affirmatively and watch the facial expressions in the room change.

Tax exempt bond financing won't work for every organization. Closing costs, minimum amounts needed to attract investor interest, governmental entity approval requirements, and financial covenants require artful navigation. But this form of financing can provide much-needed payment relief and long-term peace of mind for the nonprofit that qualifies.

CHAPTER NINE
Fundraising Management

In nonprofits, fundraising is often thought of as a necessary evil. Although the topic will be lightly addressed here, I hope you'll recognize the important cultural and financial considerations associated with managing fundraising processes in your organization. Fundraising efforts among schools and other organizations vary from a couple of annual projects to a number of small projects to an annual pledge campaign. Many organizations accomplish marketing and public relations goals through various fundraising venues, and others are focused purely on bridging the funding gap between the cost of providing services and the fees charged for those services.

The Rescue Plan Theory of Acute Pain Versus Chronic Pain

Acute pain hurts once, for a relatively short time period. But chronic pain can cripple an organization and cause negative outcomes for years. Embracing the need to address painful issues expeditiously—rather than ignoring the issue or kicking the can down the road—will reduce chronic organizational pain and its consequences.

The primary risks associated with a robust fundraising effort are organizational fatigue and cultural decline. "Here comes Mr. Smith from the school…he's probably asking for money again," is a sentiment often thought if not said among the school family. "Didn't we just have a gala?" or "Didn't we recently make a donation?" are also common sentiments among the organization's family members.

Each organization should employ fundraising methods that make sense. High-cost projects with low returns should be evaluated from a cost-benefit standpoint, and unless tangential benefits are significant, these projects should be terminated or replaced with others that are more effective. A notable exception is projects that are intended to teach stewardship and accountability. There are times, particularly in a school setting, when students learn to give time and energy for a valuable cause. I think of these as learning opportunities with a tangentially modest fundraising component—they can be important educationally and culturally; however, they may also be tedious and distracting.

The gala with a celebrity speaker or performer is rarely financially successful, but I don't discourage organizations from conducting these events if they are beneficial in other ways, such as public relations or marketing. Similarly, golf tournaments and other events tend to create noise and energy, but rarely do they raise significant funds. These events might make sense if team building, public relations, and image or brand building are among the goals for the event.

Fundraising Campaigns

The method I favor when the goal is purely to maximize income is the old-fashioned fundraising campaign. Every organization can conduct its own campaign without outside assistance, with the possible exception of campaign design and training of key personnel, which are services my firm provides. Here I'll outline the basic elements of a successful campaign.

One question that arises in schools, in particular, is who should be responsible for running the campaign or chairing the committee. This person should not be the head of school or the development director, nor should it be a faculty member or a manager. Potential conflicts of interest and a full plate of other priorities prompt this recommendation. Yes, all these people should be involved in and concerned with the campaign, but the chairperson of the campaign committee should be a board member. The committee should include the entire board, the chief executive, the development director when applicable, and various parents and others affiliated with the school family. The committee might contain a few wealthy individuals, but the primary criteria for appointing committee members include personality, sphere of influence, work ethic, loyalty to the organization, availability, and interest. A disinterested wealthy person will not be an effective team member.

Sales skills are nice to have on the committee, but an understanding of a few general sales concepts by each committee member is more important, generally speaking. The first step after formation of the committee is the building of a database of prospects. This list should include a lengthy list from each board member and other committee members. The typical committee should have twenty to thirty members, and each member should provide at least fifty and in some cases more than one hundred prospective donors. I encourage my clients to start with the success rate they expect from calls to prospects, and then I ask them to work backwards to determine the number of prospects needed to generate contacts, which generate face-to-face asks, which generate donations. Campaign committees are typically surprised at the number of prospects required given their anticipated average donation amount and expected success rate.

A good prospect list might include the following:

- School families
- Relatives of families
- Friends
- Members of churches attended by students' families
- Professionals used by families and the businesses they own, such as physicians, attorneys, and accountants
- Wealthy members of the community
- Others known for giving to similar causes

The committee should also develop a document outlining the need and explaining the case for giving. In most settings, this can be a simple one-page document. In others it might be a glossy brochure or pamphlet. In my experience, an internally prepared, professionally structured document is adequate as long as the document explains the need and the campaign details. For example, if both immediate cash and pledges are sought, the documentation should include a pledge card with alternatives for giving now and pledging over three years. In cases when building remodeling or construction is involved, artist renderings can be important.

The core of the campaign is the contact system developed by the committee. The prospect database should include names, e-mail addresses, phone numbers, and physical addresses when possible. The campaign should be announced in advance through websites, e-mail, and other media as appropriate. When the campaign begins, the chairperson should send an e-mail and a hard-copy letter to every prospective donor in the database explaining the campaign, advising the person that they will be contacted by someone from the campaign committee, and asking them to begin to prayerfully consider their gift and pledge amounts.

I favor something called "seeding the campaign" when possible. This involves going discreetly to a small group of likely donors and raising initial funds so the committee may announce "we have already raised X in cash and pledges" when the campaign is kicked off. If a new property, building, or even a new computer lab are involved, an actual physical kick-off event might occur. If the purpose of the campaign is to bridge operating cash flow deficiencies or to retire debt, a kick-off event is probably still warranted but is not as necessary.

Similarly, the establishment of a "matching fund" might be helpful when a donor or group of donors agree to fund a significant portion of the campaign goal on a matching basis. Matching funds can go a long way toward generating enthusiasm and urgency for a campaign.

Whether or not these campaign tools are used, the focal point of the campaign will be a series of in-person contacts with potential donors. Receptions or meetings may be used to invite potential donors to attend in small groups to hear the case made for giving. Personal phone calls should be used to schedule individual visits with prospective donors in most cases. It's best if the person providing the prospect can be enlisted to call the prospect to schedule the appointment. In cases involving conflicts or other sensitive issues, the development officer or a committee member might be asked to call someone from another member's list.

Use a contact management system so e-mails that start the process are followed by phone calls, which are followed by appointments, which are followed by follow-up phone calls, e-mails, and letters as appropriate. Make notes in the contact system so contacts aren't duplicated and progress is clearly documented.

Provide inexperienced committee members a telephone script, which may be developed by others on the committee. Similarly, an in-person meeting script may also be used as part of the preparation for the meeting, but a script should never be read during the meeting. It is important that each contact make an "ask"—a request to give. This should be done professionally but directly.

Sales Process Overview

A brief overview of the sales process might be helpful as background for fundraising: The sales process is simply the meeting of needs. A product or service has several component features (things the product will do) and benefits (outcomes the consumer is seeking). Consumers buy benefits, and the salesperson simply explains that the product's features provide the benefits that meet the consumer's needs. The professional salesperson then asks for the business and offers the consumer the opportunity to buy the product. Throughout the process, the salesperson might use a series of open-ended questions to learn about the consumer's unmet needs. Open-ended questions cannot be answered yes or no, and they typically begin with phrases like these:

- Tell me…
- Explain to me…

- Educate me…

- Describe…

"What are you looking to accomplish?" and similar questions are designed to prompt the consumer to describe their unmet needs. The salesperson then matches the product's benefits with these needs, explains the features, and asks for the business. A particularly effective salesperson will often not discuss price or terms until near the end of the sales process, because they realize that benefits are used to assess the real value of the product or service. The consumer is actually exchanging money for the meeting of perceived needs or desires.

The application of the sales process to fundraising isn't direct, but the two processes are closely related. I think of the fundraising ask as a wholesale transaction wherein the need is the expressed need of the organization, and the donor is making the purchase to meet the need of the organization because the need has been clearly articulated and the donor is invested in the cause of the company. I also believe the donor is meeting his or her charity, stewardship, generosity, and other personal satisfaction needs by giving.

A word about the numbers: if the committee assumes that 20 percent of those who attend receptions or consent to one-on-one meetings will give, and they calculate the average anticipated gift or pledge, it will be relatively simple to determine the number of prospects required to reach the goal. The quality of the database of potential donors, the quality of the effort to inform donors of the need, and the ability of the individuals making the ask will then be the determinants of the success of the campaign.

A word of caution: campaigns are usually more effective if face-to-face meetings are where the need is presented and the ask occurs. The campaign committee member sourcing the prospective donor should attend the meeting, and a second person, either an effective communicator from the committee or the development director, should do most of the talking. Exceptions would be close, empathetic relationships in which the committee member is comfortable asking for the donation individually. Any negative emotions, such as anger, expressed by a prospective donor are usually derived from fear. If this is encountered in any of the contact phases, it is important for the presenter to assure the person that they are simply discussing the need and will not in any way apply pressure. A good disarming statement would be something like, "I understand you don't like feeling pressured to give…none of us enjoy that feeling…we are simply providing information to the community about our project with the hopes that those who are able and willing will give, but we aren't here to pressure you into giving if you don't feel compelled to participate…We hope that one of the outcomes of our effort will be to have people like you tell us about others who might help us." Empathy statements go a long way toward diffusing negative emotions in a sales call.

A second word of caution: your organization's image is at risk with every contact made. It is imperative that committee members understand this and use the meetings to share the school's successes and strengths. The quality of education, the longevity of the organization, the awards and recognition received, and the list of colleges attended by graduates are examples of these successes and strengths. One-on-one marketing is a great way to enhance the marketing of the organization, even to those who don't give.

A final word of caution: the recession that began in 2008 damaged the American middle class. Unemployment is high, and financial difficulty is increasingly eroding consumer confidence. Unemployed, underemployed, and otherwise financially disadvantaged members of the school family will inadvertently be contacted during a campaign. When this occurs, it is imperative that empathy is expressed and pressure is not implied whatsoever. Use a statement like, "We just wanted you to know about the project, and we would welcome the opportunity to speak to anyone you know who might be interested in participating financially with us."

Ministering to all the families and individuals involved in the organization is the underlying goal of everything we do as a school or ministry. **We can't accomplish the mission, in most cases, without raising funds. It is therefore imperative that we do no**

damage to our efficacy in ministering to or serving our constituents as we pursue our fundraising goals.

A final word about fundraising: I believe the goal-setting portion of the campaign should include a stretch goal. If we must raise $700,000, then we should set a goal that is higher but still attainable. Perpetual fundraising can be tiresome to an organization, so it is important to meet the needs of the company for the pledge period plus a year or two. In a typical campaign, that means we want to meet our needs for about five years.

CHAPTER TEN
Risk Management

This is a broad topic, but here we'll focus on financial risk management. It could be argued that all risk management has financial implications.

A critical management component for any organization is its network of advisors. A good business attorney, a CPA, and other experts are important advisors for nonprofit organizations. While each of these experts will offer various services and advice, it is incumbent on the board to actually manage organizational risk. Policies and procedures and an effective management team can go a long way toward managing risk. The starting point is typically at the organizational level in the form of articles of incorporation and bylaws. Amazingly, some organizations don't take these documents seriously or refer to them when conducting business.

Insurance is a costly item often neglected by nonprofits. We will look at this item briefly; general liability, property, and directors' and officers' insurance will usually cover the basics. Other specialty or umbrella types of insurance might be necessary depending on the nature of the business of the organization. I recommend that organizations contact at least two full-service insurance brokers, discuss the business, tour facilities, and review necessary legal documents to facilitate a full insurance review. Each broker can then provide comprehensive recommendations and quotes from multiple insurance companies. Coverage limits should be adequate to replace assets in the event of loss, and deductibles should be set at optimum levels considering the organization's cash reserves, cash flow, and general financial strength. A good commercial insurance agent can recommend the most cost-effective combinations of coverage and deductibles. Boards and management must work together to use discernment regarding the allocation of available resources to meet risk management needs.

Legal compliance is more complex. This important area relates to compliance with laws, regulations, and guidelines of any governing organizations. Vigilant review is important and should be done perpetually. Accrediting bodies, attorneys, and experienced staff should be used by management to ensure appropriate legal compliance. Many organizations give their human resources officer responsibility for all compliance, since human resources compliance tends to be the most complex department in most nonprofits. Compliance should be an integral part of board discussions at appropriate intervals and documented as such in board minutes.

Self-management of risk is often overlooked. To some degree, it is possible to manage risk by accumulating cash reserves. I'm not suggesting it's possible to accumulate enough cash that the aforementioned areas of risk management are no longer necessary. But insurance deductibles can be set at higher rates—thereby reducing premiums—if significant cash reserves are present. Large cash reserves are troubling to some boards and administrators, because they believe cash should be employed toward the accomplishment of the mission. Still, a half-year of total operating expenses in cash reserves is prudent for every nonprofit organization as a hedge against potential interruptions to cash flow. Maintain additional reserves to cover capital expenditures for repair and maintenance. Stronger organizations can maintain reserves for other purposes, including scholarships and long-term growth. For smaller companies, building even modest cash reserves is an admirable goal as a start to self-managing organizational risk.

CHAPTER ELEVEN
Marketing Management

Public relations and marketing sound too abstract to many of my clients. To some degree, if we deliver our products and services at high-quality levels, the marketing sort of takes care of itself. I have several school clients that don't do a lot of formalized marketing because they have a long history of providing excellent Christian education, so the image of the organization sells itself to constituents year after year.

The Rescue Plan Theory of Marketing

The entire organization is perpetually marketing and building an image. Ignoring the simple, day-to-day marketing opportunities and thinking of marketing as just a few ads and meetings with prospective clients is failing to recognize low-hanging fruit. This fruit is typically available at relatively low cost, and yet to miss it could be very costly in terms of its negative effect on the image of the company.

My definition of marketing is much broader than advertising. My definition of marketing is the promotion of the perception of the organization to its target constituents. This definition allows the inclusion of interactions by employees at all levels, and it includes students, clients, and peripheral contacts who aren't traditionally considered part of marketing.

So marketing occurs when a neighbor attends a play or a sporting event at a school. Marketing occurs when someone walks into a school and makes a wrong turn and walks down a hallway. Marketing occurs when the phone rings and a busy receptionist answers, or when someone who isn't assigned to do so hears a phone ring and stops to answer. Marketing occurs when the basketball team takes the floor at an opposing gymnasium. Marketing occurs when a neighbor stops a parent on the sidewalk to ask how the kids are doing in school this year. Marketing occurs when an executive introduces herself to another executive in a business setting, and one executive asks the others where their kids attend school.

Marketing has more obvious, direct forms as well. Marketing occurs when the local newspaper publishes an article about a graduate of the school. Marketing occurs when an ad is placed, when prospective families visit for a tour or reception, and with every intended and unintended interaction with anyone outside the organization. Marketing is broad and very difficult to manage, and I believe it has three components: direct and indirect marketing, and culture.

Direct Marketing

Media of all types are included in direct marketing. Nonprofits use various media for promotions, so here we'll discuss concepts rather than examining every media alternative exhaustively.

I have found, both directly through our banks and by observation of my clients, that most companies rarely give marketing the appropriate level of attention. The "marketing person" is often a lower-level employee, rarely part of the senior management team. Further, marketing is thought of as something we spend money on rather than something the entire organization is perpetually engaged in. If we really believe in the broad definition of marketing, and if we include our culture as part of the delivery of our marketing to our target clients, then we should spend more time and energy on it. My recommendation for every nonprofit is that we form a culture or marketing committee, which includes the marketing person in the company, the chief executive, and others as appropriate. This committee doesn't include outside directors, but board meetings should include a report and discussion by a representative from the committee. The committee or marketing group should address all aspects of marketing the organization, including media and outlets that have been in place for some time. This evaluation should examine the efficacy and cost of all direct marketing, and to the extent possible, status quo and biases should be questioned.

Indirect Marketing

It is true that indirect or unintentional forms of marketing, such as the parents of a student speaking with others in a personal or business setting, are difficult to manage directly. However, if we include management of the culture of the organization with indirect marketing, the topic becomes more concrete. Rather than wandering through all the implications of this broad topic of culture and indirect marketing, I'm going to try to summarize a few salient concepts which I believe every organization can employ to enhance culture and indirect marketing.

The chief executive and senior management set the cultural tone. Personal communication style, responsiveness, and focus on quality are evident, and it is imperative that the management team carries the ball in this regard. The culture and indirect marketing of the organization are only as strong as the weakest member of senior management. A strong leader knows how to walk the talk while still being human and not naïve about challenges. Each member of the management team must not only know their subject area and perform at a high level, but they must also exhibit a broad sense of care and passion for the mission and quality of the organization. At the first community bank startup I worked for, the bank chairman told me that I needed to buy enough stock in the company to make me "pucker"—to cause enough discomfort at my level of investment that I would be a deeply concerned shareholder. He often referred to this as having a high "care factor."

While a nonprofit doesn't have stock ownership, it is critical to culture that the senior management team members all possess this high care factor. Care isn't something that can be feigned. Employees and constituents of all types don't often discuss this publicly, but they see through those who are just going through the motions. They also absolutely loathe executives who place their personal ambitions above the organization's objectives.

Communication reinforces culture. Positive or negative communication occurs constantly in every organization. Answering the phone promptly and pleasantly is often neglected. Automated phone systems make it difficult to reach a live person who can at least express a modicum of empathy to the frustrated caller. They are horrible enforcers of weak culture and a bad indirect marketing image. If efficiency necessitates an automated system, then the system should offer a human alternative early in the outbound announcement. Every organization can afford to have someone answer the phone by the third ring without automation. If the phone system allows, an automated feature for insiders is okay, as is a direct dial system, but for callers outside the organization, a real person pleasantly and efficiently answering the phone is a necessity.

E-mail, electronic blasts, phone messaging of all types, announcements over a public address system, the website, letters, memos, Post-It notes and all other forms of communication are indicative of organizational culture. I'm not suggesting that all these forms of communication have to be perfectly utilized, but I am suggesting that lack of responsiveness, grammatical errors, and even an unintended harsh tone can negatively affect culture and indirect marketing.

When communicating on sensitive subjects, prefer a phone call or in-person meeting. If e-mail on such a matter is necessary, it should be warm and brief. The attorney referenced in the risk management section would also recommend this approach, as written communication is "discoverable" during resolution of a conflict, and e-mail is often interpreted differently than the writer intends.

Outward impressions count. Your logo and website, as well as the condition of your buildings, grounds, and adjacent common area scream something to your target market. With the wide variety of website construction and hosting services available, budget constraints are no longer an acceptable explanation for a sloppy, tacky, ineffective website. I've been shocked to find a significant portion of my clients have websites that aren't fully functional. "This page is under construction" should never pop up on a website. Remove the link during construction, and make the construction period brief.

Please tailor the home page of your website for the general public. As you review the site, think, "What would this look like to a person outside the organization?" Then make it easy for the inquirer to get to basic information about your school or organization. Recognize that every click to every page and every photo says something about your organization. Protect the pages that talk about the lunch menu if your offerings are subpar so that only parents can see them (and then correct your offerings so they aren't subpar!).

Don't think for a second that you need to hide the fact that your organization is Christian. In fact, make it clear, and state your organizational values plainly on your website. Regardless of your target market or admission policy, your website should support the cause of Christ, and concealment of this fact can damage your culture and your marketing effort. I hear a lot of talk about "evangelistic" schools versus schools which appeal only to Christian families. While I leave such determination to the educators, it should be apparent to all of us that communication of the gospel and important tenets of the historical Christian faith is a good thing. Such communication, contrary to the lies that some have embraced, doesn't say we are hateful. Such communication says we are sinners redeemed by the grace of God, and therefore, we love all people and demonstrate that through our culture. These matters certainly require artful delivery, but a Christian organization's website should be high quality and should communicate very clearly.

My clients' campuses range from beautiful campuses with stately brick buildings and well-maintained acreage to one-story metal buildings with portable classrooms crowded onto property with inadequate parking and limited entrances and exits. Regardless of your place on this property spectrum, the way you maintain your property and signage communicates your culture to your community.

I had a boss years ago at a regional bank who would visit my branch, and he would almost always say something like, "Did you know you have a light out on your sign?" or "Your parking lot needs to be painted," or "What happened to the fence concealing your dumpster?" or "The irrigation system has stained the east side of the building," or some other maintenance item that should have been obvious to me and others. The challenge is that we see these items day after day, and we fail to notice them.

Take time to walk your campus often, and don't always walk the same route. Slow down and observe the campus from the perspective of a stranger, or if practical, invite someone from your church to tour your school campus and ask them to be aware of any maintenance or signage issues.

My clients did not become my clients because all is well financially. Most of my clients are under some form of financial pressure. Perhaps it's surprising that the condition of the properties and signs of my clients don't correlate to their financial condition, generally speaking. It is possible to maintain your property well with effort and volunteer energy if your level of care is as high as it should be.

Manage your attitude. Finally, and perhaps somewhat ambiguously to some, the way you think of your organization will influence your communication and send a message to your internal and external audiences. "We're just a poor school with declining enrollment in a poor market with high unemployment" is a theme I hear at least weekly. This isn't a necessary disclosure under any circumstance. It implies that we can't succeed because we are doomed by our environment and our current circumstances. It also tells me that leadership isn't leading with respect to the culture and image of the organization. Yes, I realize that the challenges for many of you are immense, and yes, I realize that you have been under enormous pressure for a long time now, but if you don't believe that God placed you in your environment to succeed, then, in my humble opinion, you aren't properly engaged.

An elderly lady who recently stepped down from her role as head of school now serves as vice-principal. The school is experiencing a financial crisis that jeopardizes its solvency, and enrollment has declined from about 500 to about 150 students. But her comment to me in her introduction during our initial phone contact started with, "We have a very high-quality school here, and we are a top-notch place for children to be educated." She didn't say this robotically. She said it passionately with the kind of feeling that my grandmother uses when she wants you to know she is giving you a weighty thought.

Whining and negative talk do not inspire anyone to do anything constructive. During the rest of our conversation, this dear lady was very honest about the financial issues facing the school. She wasn't blind to the very real struggles she and her school are facing. But she wanted the listener to know she is proud of the organization and its quality, and she communicated much leadership and passion in doing so.

I am not suggesting that you look yourself in the mirror and have a self-talk every day. I am suggesting that you commit to and believe in the success of your organization, and then do everything you can to positively influence the organization's culture and indirect marketing. Further, it is essential that you manage even your very senior managers with these same expectations. Culture naturally declines if leaders don't build the culture such that value accrues.

PART THREE
Thriving

JOHN WARREN

CHAPTER TWELVE
A Culture Case Study

Rick Kempton is superintendent at Annapolis Area Christian School, a three-campus, 800-student school. Rick recently moved from Southern California to Maryland to take on this assignment. He's a seasoned educator with thirty-plus years of experience. AACS had hit some bumps in the road in recent years: senior-person turnover, modest declines in enrollment, and a challenging banking relationship. Those were the primary difficulties staring Rick in the face as he arrived a couple of years ago.

Rick has a strong faith in God, and he has endured the school of hard knocks on several levels. He has survived melanoma, had numerous knee surgeries and both knees replaced in recent years, his wife is a cancer survivor, and his family has experienced other very personal challenges. Rick longs for time with his children and grandchildren who live in Southern California. He and his wife accumulate frequent-flier miles, and protect vacation time to facilitate visits across the country. Rick often communicates by phone and e-mail with his family.

Rick cries when he talks about God's grace, regardless of the setting. He does so at breakfast meetings with me privately, and he does so when he leads a chapel session full of students at his high school. Rick has been through some tough times, and he knows exactly where he is anchored by the grace of God.

I got to know Rick when a mutual friend introduced us during an Association of Christian Schools International board meeting in Orlando last year. The friend introduced us because my firm had worked on a project at his school with success, and Rick's situation, although not as dire, seemed to require similar assistance. After having met with many business leaders throughout my career, I can generally spot a senior manager with strong leadership and management skills. Rick certainly fit that description. We enjoyed getting to know each other, and I learned of the challenges at his school.

Rick is a humble man, and he will find it embarrassing that I reference him as an example of a strong leader and culture builder. Rick demonstrates all the management strengths I have outlined, but here I want to focus on culture.

I flew into Baltimore and then drove a rental car the short distance to Annapolis. The campus appeared to be in something of a residential area on a nondescript two-lane road. I arrived early for my appointment with Rick and the CFO of the school, Glen Cole. Driving onto the property, I saw that the photos Glen had sent well represented the campus. It was beautiful, with three large brick buildings separated by a commons and joined by sidewalks. Athletic facilities were adjacent, and in front of the campus was a long driveway with a nice parking lot.

Per Glen's instructions, I walked into the most prominent of the three buildings and made my way to the school office. After a very pleasant encounter with a receptionist, I sat in a common area just outside of the office. Six or seven students sat there at wooden tables in a carpeted area with an atrium feel. The students were dressed in uniforms and were all very collegial with each other. They were doing academic work, and I didn't see any faculty or staff or any other adult. I was about twenty minutes early, so I observed these students for several minutes. Then the bell rang, and the area was suddenly filled with students making their way from one class to another. The mood was upbeat, and the students were noisy but not obnoxious. Several teachers walked with students and they interacted comfortably with each other. I began to feel the culture of this place, and I liked it. I sensed that everyone wanted to be there and had a sense of comfort and pride in the school.

Rick and Glen appeared out of the sea of students and, after handshakes and introductions, they took me around the campus on a brief tour. Rick led, talking about the school from the moment we greeted each other until the end of the hour-long tour. We walked through a beautiful auditorium with students rehearsing a presentation. I could tell this tour wasn't choreographed because we seemed to interrupt a number of rehearsals and practices that were going on. We walked by a band room occupied by young high school students apparently in the early stages of learning to play their instruments. In the choral class, the leader was directing students who were standing on a riser with four rows of students—about forty kids. They were working on a few bars in a song, and the choral director had complete control. The students seemed comfortable but focused, with limited distractions (other than the three men peering into the room).

We walked to a classroom building next, and I noticed the maintenance of the grounds and buildings. This property was large and well cared for. We entered the double door at the front of the building, and I noticed that Rick knew every student we passed. He told stories of students' outstanding academic and athletic performance, and he spoke of a couple of triumphs over challenges.

A lady who appeared to be a seasoned teacher stepped into the hallway from her empty classroom. She was articulate, beaming with pride as she described the wonderful school, students, and environment. When she paused after about five minutes of monologue, I asked her if she was a teacher, and she replied that she teaches upper level math, including calculus. She might have been the school's marketing or public relations officer. This wonderful lady was authentic, articulate, and compelling in her description of AACS. Later I learned from Rick that she didn't know who we were, but recognized that we were touring the campus and wanted us to feel welcomed and informed about the culture there.

Later in the tour, we walked past the room again, and I took one step inside to find three female students there with this upper-level math teacher. She quickly said hello and pointed out that this was a tutoring group for pre-calculus. The students actually seemed to be glad to be there. They were attentive, courteous, and articulate. I felt I had entered an alternate universe of happy smart people who were staged to make my tour incredible.

When we walked into the building that houses athletics and various tangential classrooms including a large lunch area, I was surprised to see students eating lunch, walking around and talking comfortably, but conducting themselves with control and courtesy. After observing for a few minutes, I commented that it was nice to see high school students acting like young people, courteous young people, but full of youthful energy and enthusiasm. The environment was pleasant and not stifling, comfortable but controlled and contained.

Another bell rang, and the chaos of students transitioning from class to class ensued. By this point, Rick had been greeted by at least thirty students. They typically said hello or, "Hello, Mr. Kempton," and Rick typically said something like, "Hello, Steven, how did the debate go?" or, "Hello, Marsha, great job in chapel yesterday." I wondered how on earth Rick, having been on campus for less than a full year, knew so much about each of these students, faculty, and staff. I also looked at their eyes as they met, and I saw people who were comfortable and considered Rick to be their friend. They were respectful, but I could tell that Rick manages with a very warm, comfortable, engaging style. I am almost convinced that he knows every student by name, along with some of the details of their story.

One such young lady stopped to greet Rick as we were leaving the athletic building. Rick, after a short conversation, turned and said, "This is the young lady I told you about earlier, who made nationals in basketball."

I extended my hand. "Congratulations. It's nice to meet you."

Her handshake was firm, and she looked me right in the eyes (as did all the students I met that day), and she said, "Oh, thank you, sir, it's nice to meet you too."

I said something goofy about basketball, as is my practice when I don't know what to say, and she followed with more warmth and clear articulation. As we walked away, I had to ask Rick if this behavior in students is coached.

"Not really," he said. "The faculty here is amazing, and this is just the way we live."

I will not soon forget those words. He didn't say, "Yes, we beat this into them" or, "I insist on good behavior" or, "We stink now, but I'm making it better" or, "You only met the good kids…we have some real problem students" or anything of the sort. He said, "This is the way we live." That statement makes most of my points about leadership with respect to culture. Rick's attitude, his high standard for excellence, his ownership, and his personal warmth are all synopsized in that comment.

I have visited the campus three additional times and found exactly the same environment and experience. I have met the board members, and I have spent time with principals, teachers, and employees in admissions, accounting, marketing, and development. This organization has a culture that embodies the characteristics of a company that recognizes its indirect marketing is happening at all times.

AACS is a school that has enjoyed a tradition of excellence for a long time, but they are not immune from the challenges that all schools face. They have built a culture that screams excellence regardless of the adversity faced, and they inspire me to grow spiritually and otherwise.

CHAPTER THIRTEEN
The REVPASS Instrument

Seeing Financial Reality Clearly

Children are wonderful reminders of God's grace in our lives in various ways. Our daughter, Sarah, is our only child; thus, my observations are limited to my experience with her and the exchange of stories with a handful of friends. My wife and I were thirty-eight years old when Sarah was born, and we have enjoyed every moment of her childhood. I was her hero when she was young. I will never forget the shouts of "Daddy's home, Daddy's home," followed by a leap into my arms. The bedtime stories, prayers, and even the specific words I had to say when I left the room to complete the process were all so special. I remember many expressions that were special to our family, like Sarah calling Gus, our standard poodle, her "guarder dog."

She called me by my first name for about a year when she was in the fourth grade, and she told me for a number of years that she wanted to marry me when she got older. I remember her asking me to tell her stories of my childhood—she wanted me to repeat some of them night after night.

I recall discussions with my wife wherein we were so grateful that Sarah was still a little girl when some of her friends were appearing to mature at a young age. She would run and hug me before soccer practice even though some of her friends on the team thought that wasn't cool.

While I knew rationally that those days wouldn't last forever, that she would mature and possibly even stop some of these wonderful displays of affection, it seemed that everything changed suddenly at some point during her fourteenth year. Sarah is still a wonderful young lady, and she still has me wrapped around her finger. But I would be less than candid if I didn't acknowledge that I have experienced denial as she has grown from being a little girl to a young lady. At first, I didn't notice the changes. Then, as I began to notice them, I explained them away thinking that the childlike behaviors would return. Then, every now and then, if I groveled, she would accommodate me by repeating one of our family phrases from the past, and this would reinforce my ability to deny that change had occurred.

I'm now certain that Sarah is maturing into a young lady, and almost all of those adorable evidences of childhood are memories to be enjoyed but not experienced again. She enjoys time alone, and she has developed her own preferences. She makes wise decisions and informs us of fewer of her innermost thoughts. She enjoys the company of a few friends, and she prefers activities with them over time with our family alone. She is planning for college, and she has developed educational and professional aspirations largely on her own. My two years of denial are over, and I'm embracing this new reality at last. I blinked, and my adorable child grew into an incredible young lady. My processor required a couple of years to digest that fact.

Something about the human condition and the rhythm of life makes it difficult for us to see our world objectively. We embrace patterns, and we gain comfort from familiarity. I remember 2007–2008 vividly in economic terms. We had accomplished our goal of selling our second community bank at a nice profit for our shareholders, and I went through a period of assessing my career interests for the next phase of my life. My friend, Tom Coletta, urged me to meet with an old friend of mine and a couple of his associates who were starting a bank across the state from us in Tampa. They expressed an interest in expanding their business plan to include the Orlando market, so we were a potentially good strategic fit to start the bank together.

After on-and-off negotiations, we agreed to join our efforts, we executed the requisite contracts, and we began the strategic planning process. A few months later, we received a call from our case manager at the FDIC. She is a person I have known for years, and I respect her bank regulatory knowledge immensely. However, for the first time in my career, during this conversation in March of 2008, she asked us to reconsider our growth aspirations and to raise more initial capital. My reaction was that she was receiving pressure from her bosses, and she was just temporarily being more cautious.

A few months later, I learned through a friend that a large bank was selling its problem loan portfolio in its entirety for about 31 percent of the principal balance. This was unprecedented. I learned anecdotally of borrowers buying their own notes at tremendous discounts. I explained this strategy away by calling it just another example of the large banks being detached from reality. Subsequently, I learned of other banks similarly selling their problem loan portfolios at large discounts, and I noted that marginal loans were moved to the problem loan areas of a number of banks.

Then, the near-calamitous period of the third quarter of 2008 occurred, and I began to wonder about the economic environment. Even then, I explained away some of the actions taken by regulators as draconian overreactions to threats that weren't as significant as they were portrayed.

The reality that our economy and financial system were experiencing unprecedented stress finally occurred to me one night in October of 2008. We were attempting to raise more capital than we had planned on raising due to the requirements outlined by our regulators, and we held several receptions to explain our strategic plans to our shareholder base. Raising capital had been easy for us at the two previous banks, but this time, investors were more cautious. Board members who had previously estimated that we would be oversubscribed reported that their friends were not writing checks as promised. Even though our shareholders had made more than ten times their original investment if they invested in the first two of our community banks, several of them decided to reduce or cancel their planned investment in our third bank. At this point, I finally realized that the inputs that occurred during the previous year all pointed to an economic adjustment unlike anything we had ever experienced.

As I look back and, frankly, scold myself for not seeing the economic environment changes more clearly, I realize that I viewed the events of late 2007 and 2008 through the lens of our recent experience. After all, the success we enjoyed at the first two banks gave us confidence that we had figured it out to some extent. We were the best in class, and we were respected as being quite capable in our field of expertise. We had even experienced September 11, 2001, and the economic uncertainty that followed that horrible day, and we weathered that storm without losing any of the principal owed on any of our loans. Our confidence was tempered by the fact that we had endured the school of hard knocks in many respects, and we felt that we knew how to successfully manage a bank in a variety of economic conditions.

After this moment of clarity about the environment we found ourselves in, I recall that we approached our response with something of a tentative approach. In fact, we felt that we should only do the minimum necessary to strategically adjust to the environment so we wouldn't compromise our culture and our strategic strengths. We remained naïve about the adjustments required even after we came to grips with a clear assessment of our current environment.

So it is with some sense of resignation that I admit I am guilty of the tendency that people have to embrace the current way of thinking and avoid realistically viewing a calamitous situation. Only by methodically looking at objective facts over time can we react with appropriate speed to adverse changes in our environment. And our culture must include clear communication based on an environment of trust, so that bad news is welcomed as readily as positive news. How do we design processes, at least from a financial management standpoint, that provide predictive data? How do we ensure we aren't lulled to sleep by viewing input through the lens of the past?

Avoiding the Trap of Embracing the Past While Addressing Changes in Conditions

I'm an advocate of dashboard financial reports, followed by detailed financial statements and supporting reports for use by management and for board presentations. A good dashboard report should include enrollment by grade, revenue by type, expenses by type, cash on hand, delinquencies, and a cash flow summary.

Maintaining clarity so challenges can be acknowledged requires a culture that rewards disclosure—regardless of the implications of the disclosure. I have routinely heard expressions like; "I don't like surprises," "I don't handle bad news well," "I don't like to be ambushed," and the like from well-meaning managers. Worse are managers who react angrily to messengers in the organization who discover warning signs and call them to management's attention. All of these sentiments, and even our body language and facial expressions, work together to build an organizational culture that says, "don't bring me bad news." This is not only unpleasant for employees who are working hard to do their jobs while caring for the organization. It is also dangerous, and this sort of response to adverse news can build a culture that requires a sort of sugar-coating of all negative information.

Instead, negative information should be welcomed and even encouraged. A culture that encourages the communication of all issues candidly will be painful at first, and it will certainly require fine-tuning. For example, workers might tend to only surface negative information when that information is outside of their immediate area of responsibility. Employees might also develop a tendency to have a "so, what are you going to do about that," approach as they surface issues that require attention. "Catching" other employees and challenging managers can become a pastime for some, and attempts to build a culture that encourages the communication of all pertinent facts will certainly be met with some of these challenges.

Much has been written about coaching employees, about communicating clearly internally, and about culture building. Managers are often told to require employees, for example, to propose a solution when they bring up a problem or challenge. Managers are sometimes taught to require "ownership" by employees such that it is "our problem" rather than the manager's challenge to address alone. These are certainly beneficial and practical ways to encourage effective communication, but I'm advocating a cultural shift that goes beyond canned responses.

I am advocating a change in organizational culture that starts at the board level and permeates the entire organization. The change I'm advocating first requires that everyone has a general understanding of the elements of the financial dashboard. This will require some general accounting and finance education by a CPA, the CFO, or another professional. My firm often provides this education to our client organizations, for example.

The second step in building a culture that clearly identifies challenges occurs at the board level. The board must understand that we are not in an environment that only allows us to focus on hearts and rainbows. The financial management of a nonprofit is not a walk down a yellow brick road. The environment is challenging and fraught with risk, and it is important that all board members understand this fact clearly...even the glass-half-full board members who smile perpetually and exude constant affirmations.

Unfortunately, I have had to assist organizations wherein the board fired a senior executive simply because the news was bad, or because they felt like they needed to take action because the ship wasn't going in the right direction. In many cases, the new leader hired by the board is inferior from a skill set and management ability standpoint to the terminated predecessor. No, I'm not advocating a policy of retaining weak performers, but I am advocating a thoughtful approach in the conducting of the board's business such that the senior manager is comfortable and even encouraged when he brings bad news of any kind to the board.

Finally, a system of checks and balances must be put in place to ensure that financial data are considered objectively. The daily, weekly, monthly, and quarterly financial reporting that occurs in an organization must be reviewed by various people at various levels of the organization, and confidentiality must be maintained so that those outside of the "need to know" circle are not unduly alarmed or misinformed. Yes, this is challenging because the human condition features a pride problem. And yes, employees like to brag to their friends and colleagues that they have inside information. And yes, this will poison an organization if left unchecked. However, it is essential that checks and balances occur and questions are freely asked regarding the financial reporting of the organization.

I advocate dashboard reports because they contain limited information, but they tell a story if reviewed and understood consistently. I also advocate the sending of board financial reports to members at least three days in advance of meetings. While this practice can facilitate the communication of confidential data by board members to those outside the board, I believe most board members will treat the information with the appropriate level of security if properly instructed to do so. The obvious reason for the dissemination of information in advance is that we cannot expect board members to digest this important information on the fly during a meeting.

Both the weekly or monthly dashboard reports and the financial report for the board require review and cross-examination by several levels in the organization. These documents should encourage discussion and, over time, a clear understanding of the story behind the numbers should be evident to all recipients of the reports. In the section that follows, I will discuss an instrument I have developed that consolidates various financial data. This instrument should become integral to the financial reporting that occurs internally for financial management purposes.

To summarize, the following are the basic elements of facilitating the coming to grips with the fact that challenges exist in the organization:

• Create a culture that encourages the communication of challenges.

• Educate the board perpetually and agree that the board will set the tone for the welcoming of negative information throughout the organization.

• Employ a system of checks and balances to ensure that financial data are reviewed and cross-examined throughout several levels in the organization.

REVPASS — The Revenue Per Available Student Seat Instrument

I have developed this very helpful instrument as a result of the common concerns schools have with respect to comparative financial performance. Since 80 percent of the clients I work with are prekindergarten through twelfth grade Christian schools, I will explain this instrument in that context. However, this instrument may also be used by colleges and universities, and the data may be analyzed by section, class, major, and school. Most of the schools I work with are experiencing enrollment challenges and challenges in determining the appropriate amount to charge for tuition. Most of my clients also express concerns about the impact of discounts and scholarships on their solvency, but they often struggle to analyze and address these issues in the larger context of revenue management.

A note for administrators and board members of organizations other than schools

REVPASS may be used by your organization by modifying the instrument. Total available student seats may be changed to reflect your capacity, and enrollment may be replaced by total clients served. With some creativity, the instrument may be employed by almost all nonprofit entities.

Many schools are adept at expense management, but they are challenged by enrollment goals, tuition strategies, discounts, and scholarships. Further, most of the schools I work with have prescribed or target student/teacher ratios, and most of the schools have excess capacity both in terms of these ratios and physical space in at least some grades. Complicating matters further, most schools bridge the gap between the tuition paid per student and the cost of educating the student with various types of fundraising.

At some level, fixed costs in education are actually mixed, or have a fixed and a variable component, as capacity issues must be addressed to accommodate growth. REVPASS evaluates the efficiency of the organization in optimizing revenue relative to its current fixed cost structure. Therefore, it is important to consider only revenue that may be generated utilizing current facilities and faculty in the calculation of REVPASS. A helpful tool in analyzing whether or not it makes sense to hire additional faculty or incur other costs is pro-forma REVPASS. This process contrasts current REVPASS with projected REVPASS in the context of various growth assumptions.

Board members and administrators often complain that they want to serve as many families as possible, but they feel pressure to raise tuition or reduce discounts and scholarships because of the financial pressure the school is experiencing. These issues are often puzzling because of the multiple variable, simultaneous equations that must be solved. REVPASS analysis, and its derivatives EXPASS and NIPASS, are helpful tools for analyzing these multiple variable decisions.

REVPASS, EXPASS, and NIPASS are also effective indicators for comparative purposes. Specific levels, such as lower, middle, and high school, specific grades, and whole-school comparisons may be made using these tools. Period-to-period REVPASS analysis will also be an effective utilization of this instrument.

REVPASS brings together all of these concepts and consolidates them into two numbers: gross REVPASS and net REVPASS. **Gross REVPASS is calculated by this formula:**

Total Revenue ÷ Total Available Student Seats

Total Available Student Seats is calculated by examining the student/teacher ratio standard for the school as well as the physical capacity. So if the student/teacher target is 18 for a particular grade, and if the class only has 12 students, assuming that the classroom physically has an 18-student capacity, the total available student seats would be 18. If the classroom's physical capacity is 15, then the total available student seats would be 15. **Total Available Student Seats is defined as the lesser of the student number prescribed by a mandated student/teacher**

ratio and the number of student seats due to the physical limitations of the facility.

Net REVPASS is similarly calculated; however, **Net REVPASS uses revenue from tuition only in the numerator (excluding contributions and other sources of income).**

The following activities increase Gross REVPASS:

- Increases in tuition

- Increases in fundraising

- Reductions in discounts

- Reductions in scholarships

- Increases in enrollment

REVPASS is a measure of the efficacy of marketing, fundraising, pricing of tuition, and discounts and scholarship programs. REVPASS forces the spread of all revenue over available student enrollment, which allows for analysis that is more meaningful than simply analyzing revenue per actual student. This analysis will place the appropriate level of management attention on filling open student enrollment, and it will allow the board and the administration to carefully examine student/teacher ratio aspirations and tuition discounts in the context of their financial implications.

REVPASS analysis will eliminate the need to footnote changes in multiple variables, which leads to confusion for management and the board in interpreting financial data. Yes, the components of REVPASS should be analyzed independently; however, the false sense of accomplishment that can occur with other forms of financial analysis (i.e., enrollment analysis and tuition schedule increases that are negated by increases in discounts) is eliminated by REVPASS analysis. This instrument will give school leaders the opportunity to measure the efficiency of revenue production based on capacity, and it will reveal the cost of discounts in concert with the cost of less-than-optimal enrollment capacity utilization.

EXPASS is the simple calculation of Expenses Per Available Student Seat. The same "available student" determination is made in this calculation as the one we used in REVPASS. The numerator includes total expenses, and the denominator includes the number of student enrollment positions available with the limitations being the target student/teacher ratio and available physical space.

EXPASS is a tool that may be used in concert with REVPASS, but it also has efficacy as a tool to measure operating efficiency. **When used with REVPASS, EXPASS reveals the marginal income-generating capacity of the school as enrollment capacity is filled**. For example, if REVPASS is $8,000, EXPASS is $6,000, and unfilled "available student seats" total 85 for a school, the incremental income earned by filling each empty student seat exceeds $2,000. In theory, the incremental income would be the difference between the charged tuition amount less EXPASS. In practice, since some costs are mixed, a small variable cost component would impact the incremental income earned. So, if tuition charged is $10,000 per student per year, the marginal income per additional student seat filled would be $4,000 less nominal costs for supplies, curriculum, and other variable costs. Thus, in this example, approximately $340,000 (85 students times $4,000, which is the difference in tuition collected of $10,000 less EXPASS of $6,000) in income is available by filling all vacant available student seats. Again, this number would be reduced by the cost of the nominal variable costs to educate the 85 additional students.

NIPASS is Net Income Per Available Student Seat. This is simply the difference between REVPASS and EXPASS. NIPASS simplifies the interpretation process and allows administrators and board members to view specific grades or majors and their contribution to income.

Net REVPASS, EXPASS, and NIPASS analyses can be applied across all grade levels regardless of differing costs and revenue by grade level. However, the REVPASS instrument is most valuable when applied to specific grades or groups of grades such as lower, middle, and upper school grades. This is true when tuition schedules and expenses vary by grade or school. I encourage schools to employ the tool with all of the necessary, detailed inputs, but I also promote the simplification of the instrument for management purposes.

Finally, REVPASS analysis certainly has its limitations. REVPASS is clearly an income statement–focused instrument, and it doesn't contemplate items like liquid reserves and endowments. This instrument also doesn't account for unusual capacity issues, capital expenditures required to maintain property, and other balance sheet–related issues. However, in my experience, REVPASS, with its limitations, is an effective tool for measuring income efficiency, the implications of discounts and scholarships, and the cost of unfilled student capacity. REVPASS is an effective period to period indicator of progress as it is used over time, and it is also an effective tool for comparing organizations. My hope is that the REVPASS instrument will become an industry standard, and that it will be utilized to improve the efficacy of school management.

Quality and mission aspirations are integral to all of the decisions of the board, and REVPASS, EXPASS, and NIPASS analyses are simply tools to measure the efficacy of efficiency, financial management, and marketing initiatives in concert with each other. Worse than failure to implement this instrument in the financial management of a school would be its misapplication as an end-all tool for evaluating a school's performance.

Net REVPASS, revenue from tuition per available student seat, is the most valuable of the tools I have outlined in this section. EXPASS and NIPASS certainly have their limitations, but they, too, can be valuable tools. Again, peer comparisons and period-to-period comparisons are the most beneficial analyses accomplished by this instrument.

A Sample REVPASS Case Study

The following is a sample REVPASS analysis for illustrative purposes. The assumptions include a student body size of 500 with net tuition of $7,000 per student after discounts and scholarships, and gross revenue of $8,000 per student. Annual fundraising totals

$500,000, and the total available seats for the school is 580 for FY 15, and 600 for the next two years, utilizing the available student seat analysis based on the lesser of physical capacity and target student/teacher ratios.

	FY15	FY16	FY17
Total revenue: tuition[1]	$3,500M	$3,640M	$3,786M
Total revenue: fundraising	500M	500M	500M
Total gross revenue	4,000M	4,140M	4,286M
Total student seats per student/teacher ratio	580	600	600
Total student seats per facility capacity	654	654	654
Total available student seats	580	600	600
Gross REVPASS[2]	$6,896	$6,900	$7,143
Net REVPASS[3]	6,035	6,067	6,310
Total Expenses	3,400M	3,536M	3,677M
EXPASS[4]	5,862	5,890	6,128
NIPASS[5]	1,034	1,010	1,015

[1] Tuition increases 4 percent per year and student enrollment remains constant at 500
[2] Total gross revenue divided by total available student seats
[3] Total revenue from tuition divided by total available student seats
[4] Total expenses divided by total available student seats
[5] Gross REVPASS less EXPASS

In the above example, we have simplified the year over year changes such that enrollment remains constant at 500, tuition increases by 4 percent per year, and operating expenses increase by 4 percent per year. Student capacity increased by 20 from FY15 to FY16 by hiring a teacher; however, expenses still increased by 4 percent year over year.

The instrument provides various valuable data for analytical purposes, but the area of primary focus should be Net REVPASS. In this simple example, with its simplified data, we can see the value of a tuition strategy that increases actual tuition collected by 4 percent per year. We also see the value in retention of enrollment at 500, and we even see that a teacher may be added to accomplish the goal of adding a class when expenses are carefully managed.

When we stress our model in Scenario 2 below, by decreasing enrollment by 5 percent per year, note the changes.

	FY15	FY16	FY17
Total revenue: tuition[1]	$3,500M	$3,458M	$3,415M
Total revenue: fundraising	500M	500M	500M
Total gross revenue	4,000M	3,958M	3,915M
Total student seats per student/teacher ratio	580	600	600
Total student seats per facility capacity	654	654	654
Total available student seats	580	600	600
Gross REVPASS[2]	$6,896	$6,597	$6,525
Net REVPASS[3]	6,035	5,763	5,692
Total Expenses	3,400M	3,536M	3,677M
EXPASS[4]	5,862	5,890	6,128
NIPASS[5]	1,034	707	397

[1] Tuition increases 4 percent per year, and student enrollment declines by 5 percent per year.
[2] Total gross revenue divided by total available student seats
[3] Total revenue from tuition divided by total available student seats
[4] Total expenses divided by total available student seats
[5] Gross REVPASS less EXPASS

In Scenario 2, REVPASS is dropping due to the loss of enrollment each year. Because we haven't adjusted expenses or reduced teachers, our expenses remain at their previous levels. NIPASS is consequently trending downward, and unless we either resolve the enrollment runoff or reduce expenses, or both, we are going to continue to trend downward.

The REVPASS instrument is a valuable tool for modeling multiple-variable financial strategy changes including enrollment, tuition, fundraising, expenses, discounts, scholarships, student teacher ratio targets, number of teachers, and physical capacity. Facility expansion with a ramp-up period for enrollment along with expense increases may be modeled to determine financial impact. Faculty expansion may be similarly modeled. These changes may be modeled in the context of rising or falling fundraising revenue. There are a number of multivariable changes that may be modeled such that worst-case, most-likely, and best-case scenarios may be reviewed based on the best available assumptions.

Imbedded beneath the surface of our examples above are analyses of available student seats by grade as compared to enrollment by grade. Comprehensive use of REVPASS includes this analysis as various strategic and operating decisions are contemplated. Also imbedded beneath the surface are tuition discounts and scholarships offered. Comprehensive use of REVPASS would include supporting data by grade or certainly by school (lower, middle, and high), as well as discounts and scholarships. These supporting schedules will allow the modeling of changes in tuition, enrollment, discounts, and scholarships by grade.

Finally, let's review a similar spreadsheet comparing our school with two others. We will begin with assumptions for our school that we used in Scenario 1. The assumptions include a student body size of 500 with net tuition of $7,000 per student after discounts and scholarships, and gross revenue of $8,000 per student. Annual fundraising totals $500,000, and the capacity of the school is 580, using the available student seat analysis based on the lesser of physical capacity and target student/teacher ratios.

	Our School	School 2	School 3
Total revenue – tuition	$3,500M	$4,800M	$1,750M
Total revenue – fundraising	500M	500M	500M
Total gross revenue	4,000M	5,300M	2,250M
Total student seats per student/teacher ratio	580	800	500
Total student seats per facility capacity	580	800	500
Total available student seats	580	800	500
Gross REVPASS	$6,900	$6,625	$4,500
Net REVPASS	6,034	6,000	3,500
Total Expenses	3,400M	4,700M	3,400M
EXPASS	5,862	5,875	6,800
NIPASS	1,038	750	(2,300)

Our school data is taken from our first scenario. I have simplified the available student seat section such that our ratio and physical capacity yield the same output.

School 2 has 600 students and average tuition collected is $8,000. Expenses are similar to our school as a percentage of revenue; however, School 2 enjoys some efficiencies we don't have due to its size. School 2 has excess capacity of 200 students and can fill this capacity without materially increasing expenses. However, in spite of marketing efforts designed to grow enrollment, School 2 cannot seem to grow beyond 600 students. Utilizing this excess capacity is a key consideration for management going forward.

School 3 has 350 students but was once the size of our school. They have reduced tuition to $5,000 in an effort to slow their enrollment declines. But they have not reduced operating expenses because they don't want to lose good teachers or sacrifice quality in any way. Their board is gravely concerned about the future of the school, and they are pushing for dramatic expense cuts. The head of school contends that declines in quality will cause further enrollment reductions, and he feels that the board should be raising more money in donations.

Summary Comments

While we have simplified our three schools' data for illustrative purposes, there are some valuable conclusions revealed by the data. First, bigger is not necessarily better. Our school is outperforming the larger school and School 3, which is in decline. Our school's improvement will come from filling the few vacant seats we have along with management of discounts and scholarships. Our school is managing expenses well for its size, and any improvement in cash reserves will likely come from increased fundraising.

REVPASS is most valuable as a forward-looking tool for projecting financial outcomes. If the data in our spreadsheet is projected based on current enrollment and projected expenses, School 3 should immediately make expense cuts needed to balance their budget. Since our analysis doesn't include balance sheet data, we don't know how long School 3 can sustain its projected losses. But in most cases, this scenario will result in insolvency in just a few months.

School 2 has the greatest apparent room for improvement due to its excess capacity and apparently low fixed cost structure. School 2 can build cash reserves by improving per capita fundraising and filling some of its 200 vacant seats.

School 3 must balance expense cuts with marketing improvement, fundraising improvement, and tuition maximization strategies. School 3 is experiencing entity-threatening events that must be artfully managed for its survival.

Our school is performing well, and we can afford to develop long-term strategies to improve fundraising, maximize tuition, and build cash reserves.

To use this instrument effectively, build your spreadsheet and input several recent years of data. Then model projections and note the movement in Net REVPASS in particular. Change assumptions related to tuition amount, enrollment, fundraising, operating expenses, student/teacher ratios, and the like, and you will be able to begin to address policies and strategies in terms of their impact on your school's long-term financial condition. I encourage schools to engage very actively in "If…then" analysis to model tuition changes, enrollment, and fundraising in a less static environment.

Remember that REVPASS analysis is just a tool to be used in concert with other tools. Please use the contact information at the end of this book if I may assist you in applying this new industry-standard instrument.

CHAPTER FOURTEEN
Rescue Plan Summary

The Things I Often Find Myself Saying to My Clients

In this section, I will simply list several concepts that I find myself repeating to client organizations. This may seem redundant with other sections of the book, but I wanted to collect them all in one place for easy reference. Please be aware that this list is intended to provide the critical few of these items rather than a comprehensive list.

Don't abandon or water down your core values. The core tenets of the historical Christian faith, especially, must be upheld. Prayer is your most powerful tool, and it must be an integral part of the plan you put in place to recover your financial soundness.

It is never too late to resolve financial calamity. Several schools I have worked with were deeply immersed in the foreclosure process when they contacted me, and one school had already been foreclosed. No situation is too far gone, and a cursory review by a competent third party is always a prudent step.

Boards: stop behaving badly. Don't communicate covertly and tolerate conflicts of interest. Communicate at board meetings with everyone present, and know that your chief executive is on your team. Boards often split and take sides on issues that shouldn't cause division. Mature adults should be able to discuss the facts of a situation and agree on the appropriate course of action.

As a nonprofit, you are not a highly valued bank customer. It is imperative that you follow the banking advice in this book and have relationships with at least two banks. Institutional funds are available to many schools along with funding from other private sources. Explore these avenues before a banking crisis develops that limits your funding alternatives. Don't construe courtesy or sales efforts from bankers as indicating a high probability of credit approval. This industry is peculiar in that it sells first and then decides whether or not it really wants to have you as a customer.

Your financial problems will not go away until they are addressed. The root causes must be identified and dealt with. Pain is likely to be involved. In almost every case, the acute pain of addressing the problems is preferable to the chronic pain of brushing the problems under the rug. The warning signs outlined in Chapter Three should be helpful for starters, but the basic principles of financial disclosure and prudent financial management will go a long way.

The biblical principle that says debt makes one a slave to the creditor is true. Get out of debt if possible, as soon as possible. The fact that my practice focuses largely on debt negotiation, financing, and refinancing should not imply that I favor the use of leverage by nonprofit organizations. I do not believe the typical nonprofit should use debt. There are rare exceptions for opportunities with timing issues, which require loan funding for a short-term purpose and have a clearly identified source of repayment. Many organizations are burdened with heavy debt loads, and the prospect of getting out of debt in the short run isn't likely. It is for all of you that we work tirelessly to negotiate new debt terms and seek replacement loan approval. However, philosophically we oppose permanent debt for nonprofit organizations.

The Value Growth Duration Concept

Here's something for the reader who would appreciate more insight into the world of corporate financial management. This is a brief overview and doesn't get into the weeds of investment banking formulas. This concept, although not directly applicable for the nonprofit, can be a valuable tool for management as leaders look to grow the company into the future.

While Wall Street analysts go to great lengths to quantify corporate value, I don't often hear the concept applied to nonprofits. In fact, nonprofits are not really intended to build value but to provide a service. Nevertheless, the concept of value growth is one that might be helpful in the management of Christian nonprofits.

A company's value is usually seen as its perceived value to shareholders. Most analysts would say a company is valued at the net present value of its future cash flows, or said more wisely, a company's perceived value is the net present value of future cash flows as projected based on criteria the shareholders view as being realistic.

Throughout my banking career, I have often observed that most small businesses aren't really earning much of a profit or creating any sort of value for their owners. The contractor who pays his living expenses with the modest profit he earns by constructing buildings is a good example of this. After he buys and maintains tools and equipment, and given the risk inherent in the construction industry, he might earn a modest salary most years. The same is true of the franchise owner, the hardware store owner, the printer, and even the family physician.

There are notable examples, to be sure, of companies with sustainable value. Those companies are the exception rather than the rule, and they rarely sustain their perceived value over long periods of time. Many companies have cash earnings that approximate the "risk free" rate of interest they could have earned on the invested capital if they had invested in the money in a U.S. Treasury instrument or bank certificate of deposit. Therefore, I conclude that most business owners who own their own companies choose to do so because they enjoy the independence of being an entrepreneur. They might also believe they are making their world a better place, or they are otherwise fulfilling a more abstract goal, such as a childhood dream.

To build real value, however, is much more difficult. Real value growth is achieved by providing a product or service that meets unmet demands, or meets demands that were previously met less efficiently. Real value growth requires delivering a high value proposition, and this is most often done with a focus on quality.

A good example of this value growth proposition being met by different entities over the years is the cake. Back in the 1950s, the stay-at-home mother baked a cake by purchasing the ingredients, mixing the flour, eggs, sugar, and other ingredients, and baking them in the appropriate container at the appropriate heat level for the appropriate amount of time. As convenience began to surface as an unmet need, companies like Betty Crocker began to mix most of the ingredients and package them in a box. With minimal effort, additional ingredients were blended with the premixed ingredients, and the container and heat routine was repeated to produce the cake.

While these two alternatives were used for years to meet cake demand, bakeries began to meet cake demand by producing better-tasting products which were more convenient because they did all the work. Then the supermarkets caught on and began producing specialty cakes for both special occasions and everyday consumption.

While the other methods for baking a cake continue through the present time, the bakery and supermarket solution added value as the industry leader for many years. Then, Disney discovered that consumers are really looking for an experience rather than just a cake. So Disney started baking specialty cakes and serving them with their characters at parties and in their theme parks. Other companies caught on and began to provide experiences ranging from backyard party solutions to indoor play centers and others.

High-quality companies that make flour, cake mixes, cakes of all types, and provide experiences of various types for eating cake are surviving and even thriving. Others played in one of these arenas and failed. The difference is a passion for quality, which leads to innovation and perpetual revenue growth.

If the company's stock price or real market value is to continue to increase, the shareholders must be convinced that the company is growing value and that its value growth curve will continue to rise for the indefinite future. Companies go to great lengths to accomplish this perception and the cash flow reality to support it. The iPhone and all of its iterations is an excellent example of this, as are the flavors of Coke, the menu innovations at Olive Garden, and the technology advancements of GE and IBM. The value growth in these companies and many others has been sustained for long periods of time. So long, in fact, that some of them are classified as blue-chip stocks because of the stability of their earnings growth.

The value growth proposition is more difficult for nonprofits. For Christian nonprofits, only certain elements of this lesson on the duration of value growth are applicable. Biblical imperatives are much more important than anything I have to say about businesses growing value. **An organization that focuses on quality and innovatively meeting needs, whether ministry-related services or others, that are either unmet or met less efficiently, is much more likely to sustain itself financially over time.** And to be clear, when I talk about the perception of value growth, I'm not talking about marketing fluff. I'm talking about delivering at a high level and shaping perception to recognize this high level of delivery.

The stewardship and other accountability mandates from Scripture that apply to leaders of Christian organizations are more onerous than the fiduciary mandates that apply to CEOs of for-profit companies. I'm not suggesting that the mission should be compromised whatsoever. But I believe that if an organization is to sustain itself over time, it is imperative that managers focus on value growth duration in the context of the organization's mission.

Final Thoughts

I hope you'll take time to read my story at the end of this book. The reason I included it is that I want you to know that God arranged my life to have me involved in consulting with Christian schools, churches, ministries, and other nonprofits. Throughout my life, I can see God's clear direction in bringing me to this point.

I wrote this book because I see themes present in organizations across the country, and my goal is fulfilled if a section or comment creates a small change toward financial soundness in just one organization. Perhaps even a handful of the common threads and solutions that have been effective for my clients will be helpful to you and your organization.

In addition to resolving large bank debt negotiations, various financing and refinancing projects, fundraising projects, and all aspects of financial management in my consulting practice, I am privileged to work on myriad issues with organizations all over the country regarding financial matters that can determine an organization's failure or survival.

A school from Georgia contacted me while I was completing this book. They were innocent victims in a foreclosure against the owner of property they rent for their school campus. The foreclosing bank notified the school that they had until July 1 to vacate. I engaged with the school just one week prior to that date. Upon reviewing the facts, I discovered a pattern consistent with many of my clients—the bank had strong-armed the school into executing agreements, and they intended to sell the property out from under the school. They wouldn't even discuss the school's interest in purchasing the property.

I made a few very basic recommendations to the head of school, and he began to implement them. I scripted the school to prepare them for requesting a meeting with the bank CEO. And although others at the bank had denied the school this audience, the CEO agreed to meet with representatives from the school. I worked with the school to develop a document narrowing the scope of the meeting to two issues: the request to lease the property for another year, and the option to buy the property for a certain price during that year.

The CEO met with school representatives and said no.

When the head of school pressed the CEO to present the matter to his board, he agreed to do so. The head of school discussed the history of the school and its importance to the community and the families it serves as we had discussed in our preparatory session. The CEO agreed to present the request to the bank board, but he was still not optimistic as the meeting ended.

The head of school, the school family, and my family prayed that God would intervene. I was particularly frustrated by the bank CEO's response, because I knew the bank had not treated the school fairly. I had confidence that the head of school had communicated well with the CEO, but it appeared the school would have to close its doors within a week.

The head of school called the next morning to tell me that, in an amazing reversal of position, the bank sent an e-mail advising the school that they could rent the property for an additional year.

I don't know all the events that led to this decision, but I know that it is inconsistent with everything the bank had said and done over the prior eight months. I believe God answered our prayers. This small school in rural Georgia is educating children and equipping them with a Christian worldview. I get a front row seat as God works to preserve organizations across the country to accomplish the good work they are doing for His kingdom.

The war on Christianity that I refer to repeatedly is real, and it is apparent in terms of financial implications to Christian organizations. I hope this book provides insight into the bias faced by Christian organizations as they attempt to navigate the treacherous waters of financial management in this present economy.

Please contact me with your questions or individual case facts if I may be of assistance. My ministry to ministries is only as effective as my engagement with your organizations. My goal is to be used by God–through schools, churches, ministries and other organizations–to affect financial progress for His kingdom.

APPENDIX
My Story

In Chapter One, I mentioned some of the mergers and acquisitions I was involved in during my banking career and briefly alluded to a bout with cancer. Allow me to go into more detail to give you the full picture.

I grew up in Alabama and developed a love for learning early on. That came from good teachers and other positive influences. Both sets of grandparents lived nearby, and I recall their strong impact on my social and academic development.

As a child, I was socially awkward. I didn't know what to call it at the time, but I was more obsessive and more of a worrier than my friends. I worried about my family's finances, about an awful-sounding war in Vietnam, and about whether I would be able to go to college. I actually concluded—at age six—that I would probably not get to go to college.

I didn't understand the concept of small talk, and in my lower middle class environment, I didn't really have to develop communication skills. I'm the oldest of four children, and my two brothers had the charisma. My sister was the youngest, and she enjoyed lots of attention and developed more rapidly in every respect than the rest of us.

In the south, if a child expects to develop socially, he or she must play sports. I enjoyed a variety of sports, and I value the influence of coaches, teammates, and competitors which shaped me as a young man.

My first baseball practice was awkward. I was six and really didn't know whether or not I was right-handed. The glove felt strange on my left hand, and throwing with my right arm was awkward. But since Mrs. Cook, my first grade teacher, was teaching me to write with my right hand, I gave it an effort for several practices. I recall having a coach who probably resented my presence finally concluding that I was left-handed. The "must play" rules of today's youth sports league weren't in place then, but it still had to be painful to devote practice time to a kid who couldn't catch, throw, or hit. I still recall the awkwardness of learning this very difficult game. Hitting the moving ball seemed impossible, and fielding was boring. I still have deep bruises from sitting on the bench during my first two years in Little League.

My dad was hard charging and wanted me to be successful, athletically and academically. He practiced with me, and I had the good fortune, in my third year of baseball, of landing on a team with a very good pair of coaches. I began to see some meaningful playing time, which led to an improvement in social status and newfound confidence. I began to fit in with a cooler social group. Academics was a strength for me thanks to some good wiring and teachers and friends who cared enough to invest in me. Life was good.

Puberty for me and desegregation in the deep south occurred simultaneously.

Martin Luther King Jr. had marched through our little town when I was very young. I remember my mother crying and saying we had to find another route home one day because the African-Americans were marching and lying in the streets downtown. At that young age, about five, I wasn't sure what the problem was, but I could feel the racial tension. Other than limited exposure in a small convenience store my grandparents operated near downtown, I hadn't really been exposed to African-American culture.

We had a babysitter or nanny of sorts when both of my parents were working during my youth, and we sometimes drove Ruth home to the part of town where African-Americans lived. My school district was blown apart as I was set to move into sixth grade, and my school was divided. I was sent to a middle school with a student population that was 75 percent African-American.

I was stunned. Unlike my small, familiar school, this was a chaotic racial melting pot in an old, asbestos-tiled former high school building. The teachers were older and colder, and student behavior was chaotic as cultures blended. I saw my first brawl, a number of routine fist fights, and by seventh grade, I began to experience discipline from teachers and staff because I was bored and could make good grades while pursuing distractions with my friends.

Looking back, this period shaped my fondness for all types of music and culture. While I wonder what I might have accomplished academically if I had remained more focused during these formative years, I see clearly that my worldview and my ability to communicate with a broad audience were shaped by this cross-cultural experience. I recall very clearly, for example, the musical passion of our choral director, Mrs. Hardaway. Aretha Franklin, Gladys Knight, The Temptations, and The Fifth Dimension were all favorites of hers, and she and the African-American students in my school were passionate about music.

My parents took us to church sporadically, but at some point during this period, they started taking religion more seriously. We changed to a church that was more intense, and I learned that I was going to hell if I didn't "get saved." My mom talked to me about this, and a Campus Crusade for Christ person also explained it to me. I prayed a prayer as I was asked to, and I was baptized. Because I was about eleven years old, I didn't notice a radical change in my life, but my family took church, the Bible, and matters related to God more seriously. I became confused about theology, but people called me a Christian and called the experience my salvation. That worked for me, and church was added to sports and academics on my list of important things.

Like others, we moved to a nearby town to escape the declining school system, so I started ninth grade at a new high school. Puberty was on full throttle at this point, but I wasn't sure what to make of it. If my parents had a birds-and-bees conversation with me, I missed the point of it. I relied on a couple of older friends who walked me through the details of sex and all things female. This proved to be a distraction a couple of years later, but I was still a good kid with strong academic performance.

Football was brutal. Baseball seemed much more predictable and civil, but football was the preferred sport for boys. It took years of training to hit other players hard. Unfortunately, in both ninth and eleventh grade, my playing was hindered by injuries, and although I demonstrated potential, my football career didn't blossom. Sports, girls, music, and partying were my focus during high school. My relationship with my parents began to deteriorate, as did my conduct and focus on healthy objectives.

I'm envious of those who maintained more order than I during the transition to college. Because of the distractions I chose, I don't believe I was as socially mature as my peers. I experimented with alcohol and other unhealthy pastimes. I realized that wealth, privilege, and opportunity were not mine, and I felt a deep sense that I would never dig out of the hole I found myself in. It wasn't until years later that I saw what progress toward escaping the chains of socioeconomic depravity might look like. My experiences to this point left an indelibly scrappy etch on my DNA.

One skill I developed was manipulation. I thought living life transparently resulted in trouble at every turn, disappointing my parents and facilitating bad outcomes of all sorts. Pretending to be the right person in each situation was much more productive. Truth rarely entered my thinking—I was much more concerned about getting the desired outcome.

I didn't know who I was, what I believed, or what I was even interested in.

I liked whatever I needed to like to impress the audience at the time. My goal was to survive without offending others. I walked down the middle of almost every issue. I lied routinely if I thought a situation warranted it to maintain the status quo. I had learned as a child to hate conflict, and I would sell out in a heartbeat to avoid it.

I couldn't square the theology I had learned to this point with the Bible, and I didn't really see any sort of harmony in any area of my life. I focused on graduating from college, getting a job. I could figure the rest out later. Although I affirmed that I was a Christian, I didn't really understand what that meant in terms of my life and decisions.

Outwardly I conformed, while inwardly I was an angry, rebellious, miserable, confused, immature young man.

Looking back, I'm grateful for some of that pain and confusion, because it prepared me for what would happen later.

My professional and married life began at about the same time. Thankfully, God saw fit to have my friends introduce me to the most beautiful and kindest young lady I had ever met. Connie is not only physically beautiful but has a sense of inner beauty that comes from a close walk with God. Uniquely incredible in every way. We fell in love and were married the following year.

My career experienced several phases. After receiving a business degree, I worked as a CFO for a couple of companies. I continued my education with an MBA degree from the University of West Florida in Pensacola.

During my final year in this program, a CPA friend introduced me to the manager of Chase Manhattan Bank's Pensacola loan office. This friend and a professor of finance in my MBA program were influential in connecting my aptitude and interests with banking. I owe each of them a great deal of credit for insightfully nudging me in that direction.

My Banking Career

My journey was not without ups and downs. Chase closed its Pensacola office after a couple of years, and I found myself in Morristown, New Jersey, thanks to a couple of senior executives at Chase who rescued me from the Pensacola shutdown. I spent the following year or so sharpening my credit skills and learning from experienced bankers. I learned the New York banking culture and often was able to accompany my boss to high-level meetings. I learned how to dress, speak, write, and talk like a banker, and I learned credit analysis across a broad spectrum. This experience proved very valuable throughout the remainder of my career.

I have always had a strong fear of failure, and a reciprocally strong drive to succeed. Because I underachieved academically while working on my undergraduate degree, primarily due to a lack of focus, I was at a loss to explain my much stronger academic performance in graduate school as well as my early career success. It wasn't until I went to work for a large regional bank back in Florida that I learned more about my intellectual ability, personality type, and management style.

I was contacted about a promotion opportunity after just a few years at the regional bank, and after a successful interview, I learned that a day of testing with an industrial psychologist was part of the hiring process.

I approached testing day with trepidation and a sense of going through the motions. I was concerned that I needed a positive outcome, and this process was pass-fail as far as I was concerned. The psychologist explained the day's agenda and started me on a series of tests that left me mentally drained a few hours later. Then he interviewed me for two hours, and he sent me back into the testing room for several more hours.

While I couldn't be certain, my impression was that my IQ, sales aptitude, communication style, management style, personality, and organization skills were all strenuously tested. The tests were strictly administered and timed, and the final exercise was an "in basket" test. I received a stack of papers, a pen, and a note pad. I was told that the office had just closed and I had to leave for a flight in just 45 minutes. I had to go through the basket and leave notes for my assistant to use the following morning. This exercise delivered the knockout punch the rest of the day set me up for. I was exhausted, the directions were only as clear as outlined above, and I left feeling I had bombed.

Amazingly, a few days later my new boss called and congratulated me. The promotion was mine, and the bank would give me a relocation package to move me to my new town near Tampa. He said I had performed well, and the psychologist would contact me to review my results. Bob added that he had completed this same day of testing not too long before, and he found the review of the detail to be "off base" as far as the psychologist's summation of his strengths and weaknesses. I consequently thought little about this review until the day arrived about a month later when the psychologist arrived at my office with a detailed report.

Several events in my life and career stand out in terms of significantly shaping me: the date I truly became a Christ follower, my marriage, the birth of our daughter, and a handful of others. I didn't expect my debriefing with Dr. Lister to be that significant, but I received information that day that dramatically changed my career and the way I viewed myself.

Dr. Lister summarized the feedback, describing me so accurately that I began to rethink my expectations. Then he dropped the bomb: my IQ is very high, and he said I'm bright enough to reach the highest levels of banking.

Although I had enjoyed academic success when I put forth the effort, and I had enjoyed a modicum of early career success, I had no idea my intelligence was even above average. And I questioned whether I had what it takes to carve out a successful banking career.

Dr. Lister explained each individual component of all the tests. He made perfect sense, but I had to ask at the end of the session if he was certain he had the right guy. My confidence was not, and sometimes is not, commensurate with the feedback I had received. In fact, I was insecure and had developed a pattern of looking for affirmation in a hypervigilant way as I took one cautious career step after another. That session, along with a four-page letter he left with me, provided perspective that later allowed me to replay parts of my life with a clearer understanding of my strengths, weaknesses, and outcomes.

I didn't immediately grasp all the information Dr. Lister provided, and frankly, it wasn't until I was being recruited by another bank and had to endure a similar battery of tests with very similar outcomes that I became convinced that I was bright and capable. Those attributes didn't fit my self-talk narrative. Complicating the matter was my lack of confidence and even twisted thinking that I had developed as coping mechanisms during my youth.

In the middle of my banking career, God used a series of events, a career setback, input from my wife, my own confusion, and a good pastor to make me address my regeneration and its authenticity. I realized that despite understanding key biblical concepts, I had no confidence that my faith was authentic. I had served as a deacon, been involved in Bible study, and lived a double life of worldliness. I was guilty and hurting as I looked at my real spiritual condition.

I visited my pastor friend, Keith Reece, and experienced another significant moment. He explained very clearly that the gospel of Jesus Christ is about God's promises and His character rather than our own performance. I didn't think for a second that I could be good enough to deserve to be called a Christian, but I did believe I could follow the Bible's prescription for becoming a Christian if I had the right thoughts and prayed the correct version of the sinner's prayer.

To this day, my study of theology is a source of comfort and strength—even in the face of my own bad thinking and guilt—because I recognize that God is the focal point. He is the one who is powerful and loving, and He does the saving. My role is to trust Him, to repent and have simple faith in Him. What a beautiful concept. Now I understand that Jesus Christ is the nexus of a much larger story than I realized as a young adult. God reached down to sinners by sending His Son to become sin for us, and in His death on the cross, He forever satisfied God's perfect righteous requirements on our behalf (2 Corinthians 5:21). He lived a perfect life, died, and was resurrected on the third day (1 Corinthians 15:3-4). We simply believe on and trust in Him to save us as we repent of our sins. We recognize that we cannot save ourselves, and lean completely on Him for salvation.

My life didn't change overnight, and I frankly cannot be certain that my childhood conversion experience wasn't authentic. But I began to think differently about my life and my sin, and took an interest in going to church, reading books about faith in God, and learning key elements of Scripture. My appetite for learning about theology was insatiable. I ordered books and tapes, and I began to wake up an hour or two early each morning to study the Bible and read related books. I even listened to compact discs with Christian conference and teaching session recordings in my car. God was clearly at work in me.

Connie gave birth to a beautiful girl after several failed attempts resulted in miscarriages. Our daughter, Sarah, was born after we had been married eighteen years. She is now fifteen years old, and she has my wife's beauty and the godly character I saw in Connie when I first met her. God's blessing and grace are present to me every day through these two women.

At about this time I transitioned into the world of community banking from regional banking. Simply put, a community bank is a small bank capitalized by local individual investors, whereas a regional bank is a multistate bank capitalized with institutional capital (think Wall Street) and traded on a stock exchange.

Charlie Brinkley was the chairman of my first community banking effort, and he and John Squires, the bank's CEO, taught me much about the banking industry that my years of regional banking experience didn't. It took quite a leap of faith for John and Charlie to make me president of their Central Florida bank charter.

Another Important Aha Moment...

During the interview process, Charlie looked at me across a small table in John's office, and said, "Now we want you to invest in our stock if you're going to work here. We want all our key people to be shareholders."

My first thought was, *Wait a minute…I have to buy stock in this bank to work here?* I reflexively asked, "How much stock are you expecting me to buy?"

Before the *y* sound had ceased, Charlie said, "Enough to make you pucker."

I said, "Pucker?"

And Charlie said, "You know, that feeling at night that you have when you're lying in bed staring at the ceiling fan…that's puckering."

I said, "What if $20,000 makes me pucker?"

Again, without hesitation, Charlie said, "I don't care if it's $20,000, $200,000, or some other number, we just want our key people to own stock in the bank."

In an amazing display of all the selling skills I possess, I convinced my friend Tom Coletta to leave the friendly confines of the regional bank and join me in my new community banking effort. Tom is a can-do, grab life by the horns sort of guy. He moved to Florida from New York a few years earlier and quickly became the best commercial lender in my group at the regional bank. In addition to looking like a business version of Donny Osmond, Tom is articulate, very smart, and has a way with people. His natural sales skills are amazing.

Tom joined the community bank with me from day one, and he responded to Charlie's "enough to make you pucker" edict with, "I'm all in…I want to buy $250,000 of the stock…This is exciting."

As we left the office, I asked Tom where he was going to come up with $250,000, and he said, "I already researched it…they have a correspondent bank that will loan me the money." So Tom borrowed most of the $250,000.

My pride wouldn't allow Tom, ten years my junior, to show me up by investing more than I did. So to match Tom's investment I borrowed from my 401(k), and Connie and I invested our entire life savings in the bank.

On the personal front, my wife and I were growing spiritually and began attending a new church regularly. We began tithing— that is, giving the church 10 percent of our earnings—and became members. Our daughter was three years old, and she began learning about God through classes for children her age.

Looking back, I can see very clearly that God was preparing us for an event that would rock our world like no other. Although we can't see every detail clearly, and we certainly don't understand God's purposes completely, I have complete clarity about this period of spiritual preparation.

The first community bank sold just four years after its founding, and investors made an average of about four times their initial investment, depending on their purchase date and commensurate stock price. The process began with my boss, John Squires, calling me into his office to tell me that an acquiring bank had expressed interest in our bank. He said a team of about thirty people would arrive over the upcoming weekend, and he asked me to coordinate some of the elements of the process. He stressed confidentiality, and he seemed confident that this might be the transaction we had all been hoping for.

Personal Crisis—All Things Work Together for Good...

Rob was our senior real estate lender, and he had just turned fifty years old. One day, without any sort of provocation, I felt compelled to go down to his office to ask him about a colonoscopy he had just completed. He told me about the process, and he gave me a note with his gastroenterologist's name and phone number. He told me we really don't need to have this procedure done until we turn fifty, and I certainly didn't need to do so at age forty-four.

When I walked back to my office, I walked past my assistant's desk and heard a tone of frustration in her voice as she spoke on the phone. I continued into my office, but when the conversation had ended, I asked her if everything was okay. She was excellent at handling people of all types, so the conflict must have been serious.

Larry, a long-time customer and friend, was selling a piece of commercial property. The complexity of the transaction called for a partial release of mortgage. Since neither she nor Larry fully understood the process or the approval the bank had already put in place to accommodate the transaction, the conversation had been awkward and tense.

I collected the facts and called Larry immediately. We resolved the business issues quickly and amicably. Based on Larry's weak-sounding voice, I asked if he was okay. We were not best friends, but we were close enough to have shared Orlando Magic game tickets, and we had done a significant amount of business together as our companies grew over the years.

Larry's response, in the context of my visit to Rob about his colonoscopy, was a game changer. He said, "I'm about to die from this colon cancer." When I questioned further, he said he had tried to keep the matter private because he had successful surgery four years earlier, after the original diagnosis. When I asked how he went from successful surgery to terminally ill, Larry said he had declined the recommended chemotherapy regimen because of an acute fear of needles. When the cancer recurred, Larry agreed to do the chemo, but the cancer had spread to other organs and treatment was ineffective.

I told Larry I was shocked and sorry. After I hung up, I called Rob's gastroenterologist and scheduled an appointment for the following Tuesday.

Our potential merger partner's due diligence went very well, and John Squires said the deal was going to happen. Several of us spent the next few days calculating the implications on our stock holdings. I was grateful for Charlie's insistence that I invest, and I was also grateful that Tom Coletta set a high bar. While the deal we structured had many variables, I knew Connie and I would receive about a million dollars based on our stock holdings.

I was invited to a meeting of about twelve people at Orlando Executive Airport the following week. The meeting included senior management from our bank and the acquirer so we could discuss the transaction and begin getting to know each other personally. This was a Thursday morning in March, 2004. My gastroenterology appointment was scheduled for Tuesday of the same week.

I arrived at the gastroenterologist's office on time, having completed the lengthiest medical history questionnaire I had ever seen. The doctor was kind but quirky, and he spent about five minutes with me in his office, the type with a desk and chairs for guests. He asked if I had any symptoms of difficulty with my colon. When I told him I might have a hemorrhoid, he asked whether the bleeding was red or dark. I told him I had no abdominal pain and that the small amount of blood I observed was red. I added that just three months earlier, I had a physical with my family doctor which included a fecal blood test which was negative.

He laughed and said, "Well, you don't have colon cancer, but since you seem to be concerned, let's do a colonoscopy to be certain." His assistant scheduled the colonoscopy for Monday of the following week at Florida Hospital, where my wife served as director of children and women's services for a number of years. I took home a prescription for the drugs for "prep day," the awful day before the procedure during which the contents of my intestines would be completely emptied to prepare a clear canal for the six-foot hose with a camera on the end.

I returned to the office and attempted to do business as usual in the days prior to the Thursday meet and greet. Between the chaos of the merger and my fear that my colonoscopy wouldn't go well, I was very emotional. I asked Connie about colon cancer, and I could think about little else.

At the covert meeting with our acquiring bank, I experienced something of a panic attack. I couldn't hear the speaker, and I began to feel my heartbeat and respiration racing. This feeling was so overwhelming, I went into the hallway and called Connie on my cell phone asking her if she could move my colonoscopy from its scheduled day the following Monday to Friday—tomorrow!

She said that would be impossible, because I hadn't started the prep, but she agreed to call to placate me. Amazingly, the gastro's office had an opening on Friday. I needed to go home immediately to start the preparation. The office provided modified instructions, since I had not started the day-long cleansing.

The process was not horrible, but it wasn't pleasant by any means. When we arrived at the hospital, my overwhelming sense that something was wrong with me continued, and I asked my wife to be sure to share the results very plainly with me. Connie is a sweet person who is very concerned about the happiness of everyone around her, and I didn't want her to sugarcoat my diagnosis, since I thought I would be hearing it from her.

In 2004, the drug of choice for sedation of this type was Versed, a mind-erasing drug that makes a person's memory malfunction so the discomfort of the procedure is forgotten. Since physicians are aware of this, they talk to a family member about the outcome of the test. Thankfully, new drugs with shorter half-lives are now used for sedation in almost all colonoscopies and similar procedures.

Connie told me when I awakened from the colonoscopy the following day that the doctor was stunned to find a "golf-ball-size tumor" in my sigmoid colon. Unfortunately, she had to tell me about ten times because I would fall asleep, awaken, and ask for the outcome over and over because of the effect of the Versed.

I remember us crying together in the recovery area, and I remember a very sweet nurse stopping at my bed and saying, "I was in the room with you when your colonoscopy was done, and I want to tell you this is not a death sentence. You have a good chance for survival because of the type, size, and location of your tumor." Both she and the doctor indicated the tumor was very likely to be cancerous, but this would be confirmed by a tissue sample, which was sent to pathology. A blood test was immediately ordered, and a CT scan was scheduled for the following Monday.

Just over six months later, I had completed three surgeries and a six-month chemotherapy regimen. The life-changing impact of coming to grips with one's mortality, along with the spiritual and emotional implications of this, is too broad and weighty for a discussion here. Please indulge one brief anecdote which perhaps will provide a glimpse of some of the challenges our family experienced during this time.

Communication is challenging at best for me. I often assume that others are on the same page with me only to determine later that this wasn't the case. Communication about cancer is exponentially more challenging. Well-meaning people don't know what to say. Life goes on and the mundane continues, creating awkward judgment calls about whether or not to mention cancer or the treatment. Worrying about the effect of the situation on close family members is overwhelming. At times, the immensity of the diagnosis is more than a person can bear. Watching a news story about a celebrity who just died from your type of cancer is incredibly jolting. Trying to trust God when dealing with crisis after crisis is challenging and even confusing. I didn't question, "Why me?" but I did wonder about the future, and I wanted to see God's hand of comfort and grace more often.

Our daughter was just five years old when I was diagnosed with stage three colon cancer. She was in first grade. Sarah has always been a thinker—very smart and very compassionate. She has from an early age had incredible communication skills. My first lucid thoughts after my diagnosis went immediately to her. I wanted to see her grow up. I didn't want this trauma to invade our family.

In one of our earliest conversations after the sedation wore off, Connie and I discussed the potential effect of this diagnosis on Sarah, and we decided to tell her I had an illness requiring surgery and strong medicine. We decided not to use the word *cancer*, and we decided not to call the treatment *chemotherapy*. Otherwise, we were transparent about the seriousness of the situation, but we often told her that I would be okay after the surgery and medication. We made this decision because, like me, Sarah can be a worrier. We tried to find balance between giving her enough information and alarming her.

My chemotherapy side effects included cold dysesthesia, a condition that makes touching or tasting anything cold very painful. So I couldn't drink cold beverages or even reach my hand into a refrigerator. Thankfully, we live in Florida, and the weather was warm during the spring of 2004. Probably the most challenging part of my chemo regimen was tiredness, stomachaches, and drinking only warm beverages. Cold water is amazingly tasty after we're deprived of it for even a short time.

I didn't realize how much I missed swimming in our pool with Sarah. So when my last chemo treatment ended and the side effects dissipated, I asked if she wanted to go for a swim. Connie and I had both experienced a sense of guilt from not telling Sarah the whole truth about my diagnosis, and since I would be tested for recurrence often, we knew the subject wasn't going to go away. We decided I would tell her while we were swimming.

I started the conversation with, "Sweetheart, there is something I need to tell you related to my surgery and medicine."

Sarah interrupted me. "Dad, is this about cancer?"

Needless to say, a blunt object across the head wouldn't have stunned me more. "You know about cancer?"

"Yes, I've known all along, but I thought you and Mom were worried about it and didn't want me to know, so I didn't mention it."

I asked how she knew.

She said, "Remember Grandma and Grandpa staying with me while you were in the hospital? Well, they thought I was asleep, and they were talking in the family room…You know they talk loudly because they don't hear so well. And they mentioned cancer. I could tell they were really worried about you, but I didn't really know what cancer is. I know now because I asked some of my friends."

That was a projectile tear moment for me. I hugged her and explained why we hadn't used that word. She said she understood, and that she wasn't worried because she trusted God would take care of me.

I don't know that I have ever been brought to my knees so quickly. My daughter overheard my precise diagnosis, and she didn't want to alarm Connie and me because she knew we had a lot of emotional issues to address. And she only discussed it with me when she knew the subject was no longer out of bounds.

God works through our children so often to teach us valuable lessons. This interaction, and the entire cancer diagnosis and treatment experience, provided me with one valuable lesson after another.

Among other things, cancer taught me to slow down and enjoy the process and people. It taught me very clearly that eternity is far more important than the temporal pursuits that had been my obsession. It taught me that death and illness are real concepts. It taught me that the decision to trust in Christ for salvation is the single most important decision a person can make. It also taught me that the trivial cares of this world are indeed trivial.

The initial diagnosis, subsequent testing, and various treatment for all types of cancer are daunting. God used these experiences to awaken me to the urgency of living life seriously with eternal objectives in mind. My focus on following Christ increased and has continued to grow. In a very real sense, I'm grateful for this experience. I wouldn't have chosen that path, but I don't think I could have learned the profound lessons God taught me any other way.

Leaving Banking

The bank that acquired our first community bank was subsequently acquired by a much larger regional bank. This announcement occurred during my chemo treatment. Near the end of my regimen, Tom asked me and three other bankers if we would consider moving to a new start-up banking effort. We analyzed the opportunity, and community bank number two was born. This bank was acquired by a larger bank just two years later. The transaction was very profitable for our shareholders, and the acquiring bank required several of our senior managers to execute long-term employment agreements as part of the transaction.

I was contacted by my friend Charlie Allcott the day the acquirer of our second community bank announced they would be selling their bank to a very large bank from Canada. After months of negotiating and analyzing, Tom and I decided to join Charlie and his team in starting this new bank. The economy began to change in late 2007, but we were confident of our ability to manage a bank and create shareholder value, so we pressed ahead.

144

Raising capital in 2007 and 2008 wasn't easy, but we successfully raised $56 million. Our regulators were amazed and pleased, and we began building branch offices and hiring bankers. We reached profitability very quickly, and we were able to grow the bank, more methodically than our previous efforts but successfully, during the following three years.

Tom left the bank at this point to pursue an entrepreneurial opportunity outside of banking. His leaving left a large hole in the organization and in my heart. I missed my friend on many levels.

The pressure on banks from regulators, the economy, and shareholders was dramatically more intense than in all my previous years of banking. We employed a team of good bankers and board members, and thankfully we weathered the storm quite well.

In the summer of 2011, a bank asked if we would be interested in merging. This was amazing because there had been no whole-bank transactions in Florida prior to this for several years. There were plenty of failed bank acquisitions, but we were healthy and didn't think ourselves attractive to a bank as strong as that one. We negotiated preliminary deal terms and requested regulatory approval. The process of due diligence and all other aspects of the merger went incredibly smoothly. This astounded even our attorney, who often had conversations with me about the incredibly low probability of putting a deal like this together in this environment. This transaction was also peculiar because our acquirer was probably the strongest bank in Florida in many respects. The top three executives are legendary in Florida banking, and they could pick and choose their acquisition targets at will. I would have put them at the end of a list of banks that might have been interested in acquiring ours. In fact, I might have declined to prepare such a list, because in my mind the probability of such a transaction was near zero.

During this time, I began experiencing a strong desire to leave banking and do something more meaningful with the rest of my life. I read several books on the topic of changing careers, and I prayed for God's direction. I sought the counsel of friends and ministry leaders, and I began to quietly inquire about opportunities in ministry-related fields for someone with finance experience.

Then I visited the Association of Christian Schools website, looking for whatever finance-related openings I could find. That led me to Aurora Christian School, and to a consulting career I could never have planned without God's guidance and inspiration.

Overwhelmed? We Can Help.

CFS Financial works with Christian schools, churches, ministries, and for-profit businesses to restructure, negotiate, and refinance debt. We also have specialization in strategic planning, fundraising, budgeting, and all aspects of financial management.

John R. Warren, the founder of CFS Financial, has twenty-eight years of commercial banking experience, including service as board member, chairman, CEO, and president of three community banking companies. His passion is using his skills, experience, and education to advance Christian education and the work of churches and parachurch ministries. He has provided consulting to schools, churches, and ministries nationwide.

Learn how our services can help you get on the path to healing, solvency, and financial success. Visit cfsfinancial.net for more information or contact John R. Warren directly: jwarren@cfsfinancial.net.

52757921R00091

Made in the USA
Middletown, DE
21 November 2017